Praise for HUNDREDS OF HEADS™ *Survival Guides:*

"A concept that will be... a huge seller and a great help to people. I firmly believe that today's readers want sound bytes of information, not tomes. Your series will most definitely be the next 'Chicken Soup.'"

—CYNTHIA BRIAN
TV/RADIO PERSONALITY, BEST-SELLING AUTHOR: CHICKEN SOUP FOR THE GARDENER'S SOUL; BE THE STAR YOU ARE!; THE BUSINESS OF SHOW BUSINESS

"Move over 'Dummies'…Can that 'Chicken Soup'…Hundreds of Heads are on the march to your local bookstore!"

—ELIZABETH HOPKINS
KFNX (PHOENIX) RADIO HOST, THINKING OUTSIDE THE BOX

Advance Praise for

HOW TO SURVIVE A MOVE

"How to Survive A Move is full of common sense ideas and moving experiences from every-day people. I have been in the moving industry for 22 years and I was surprised at all the new ideas I learned from your book!"

—FRED WALLACE
PRESIDENT, ONE BIG MAN & ONE BIG TRUCK MOVING COMPANY
WWW.ONEBIGMAN.COM

"I've been in the real estate business for 29 years and I thought I'd heard it all—until I read this book! I loved it and learned a few things myself! I will definitely recommend *How to Survive A Move* to all of my clients."

—CHERI HURD
PRUDENTIAL COLORADO REAL ESTATE

Praise for other HUNDREDS OF HEADS™ *guides:*

HOW TO SURVIVE YOUR MARRIAGE

"Reader-friendly and packed full of good advice. They should hand this out at the marriage license counter!"

—BOB NACHSHIN
CELEBRITY DIVORCE ATTORNEY AND CO-AUTHOR OF I DO, YOU DO . . . BUT JUST SIGN HERE

"Full of honest advice from newlyweds and longtime couples. This book answers the question–'How do other people do it?'"

—ELLEN SABIN, MPH, MPA
EXECUTIVE DIRECTOR, EQUALITY IN MARRIAGE INSTITUTE

"A unique offering, and sorely needed resource, of advice and wisdom from men and women who have found creative solutions to the many challenges of marriage and now are reaping its rewards."

—MARCIA NADEL, JD, MFT (MARRIAGE FAMILY THERAPIST)

"How to Survive Your Marriage is a fun companion to research-based marriage manuals. Great for starting a discussion with your partner or laughing at the commonality of concerns that engaged couples often face."

—DRS. PATRICK AND MICHELLE GANNON
PSYCHOLOGISTS/COUPLES EXPERTS AND FOUNDERS OF MARRIAGE PREP 101

"This book is the best wedding present I got! It's great to go into a marriage armed with the advice of hundreds of people who have been through it all already!"

—ANN MEAGHER
MARRIED 2 MONTHS

"Congratulations! What a great idea. My wife and I (95 and 96) don't intend to quit after 71 years of marriage--it's a great institution. This book should help lots of other people match our record."

—DAVID COHEN
EXECUTIVE DIRECTOR, FRIENDS OF QUEENS COLLEGE (NY) LIBRARY
MARRIED 71 YEARS

HOW TO SURVIVE YOUR BABY'S FIRST YEAR

"An amazing kaleidoscope of insights into surviving parenthood, this book will reassure moms and dads that they are not alone in the often scary world of bringing up baby."

—JOSEF SOLOWAY, M.D., F.A.A.P.
CLINICAL ASSOCIATE PROFESSOR OF PEDIATRICS
WEILL MEDICAL COLLEGE OF CORNELL UNIVERSITY

"What to read when you're reading the other baby books. The perfect companion for your first-year baby experience."

—SUSAN REINGOLD, M.A.
EDUCATOR

"Full of real-life ideas and tips. If you love superb resource books for being the best parent you can be, you'll love *How to Survive Your Baby's First Year.*"

—ERIN BROWN CONROY, M.A.
MOTHER OF 12, AUTHOR, COLUMNIST, AND CREATOR OF TOTALLYFITMOM.COM

HOW TO SURVIVE DATING

"'Be yourself' may be good dating advice, but finding Mr. or Ms. Right usually takes more than that. For those seeking more than the typical trite suggestions, the new book *How to Survive Dating* has dating tips from average folks across the country. It's like having a few hundred friends on speed-dial."

—KNIGHT RIDDER/TRIBUNE NEWS SERVICE (KRT)

"Great, varied advice, in capsule form, from the people who should know--those who've dated and lived to tell the tale."

—CARY TENNIS
COLUMNIST, SALON.COM

"A wonderful book, with thought-provoking advice--I'm going to recommend it to all my members. It gives valuable perspectives from others in the dating world. A one-stop shop for dating tips!"

—SARAH KATHRYN SMITH
OWNER, EIGHT AT EIGHT DINNER CLUB--A BETTER WAY TO MEET!

"Reading this book, I laughed out loud and also got randomly offended, depressed and even inspired. . . . A most superior art form for dating manuals."
—*The Courier-Journal (Louisville)*

"Reading *How to Survive Dating* is like having a big circle of friends in one room offering their hard-earned advice about the toughest dating dilemmas. From the first kiss to knowing when it's time to say 'I love you,' this book can help you avoid the headaches and heartaches of dating. *How to Survive Dating* is a must-read for singles."
—*The Waukon Standard (Iowa)*

"Hilarious!"
—*Teena Jones*
The Teena Jones Show, KMSR-AM (Dallas)

HOW TO SURVIVE YOUR FRESHMAN YEAR

"An amazing collection of tips, stories and fun. A *tour de force.* A great send-off for every high school senior."
—*Jeffrey P. Kahn, Ph.D*
Professor, University of Minnesota, Director, Center for Bioethics

"If only there had been a guide like this when I went to college, I could have avoided a lot of mistakes."
—*Leslie Gilbert-Lurie*
President, Los Angeles County Board of Education

"Explains college to the clueless . . . This quick read is jam-packed with tidbits."
—*College-Bound Teen, Spring 2004*

"A fun book. . . A plethora of candid suggestions. . . helps new college students get a head start on having a great time and making the most of this new and exciting experience."
—*College Outlook, Fall 2004*

"Questions are addressed with honesty and humor. This would be a great book to have for the graduating high school seniors to make them less anxious about college."
—*MLS Ingram Library Service 'Hidden Gem', July 2004*

How to Survive A Move

WARNING:

This Guide contains differing
opinions. Hundreds of Heads
will not always agree.
Advice taken in combination may
cause unwanted side effects. Use
your Head when selecting advice.

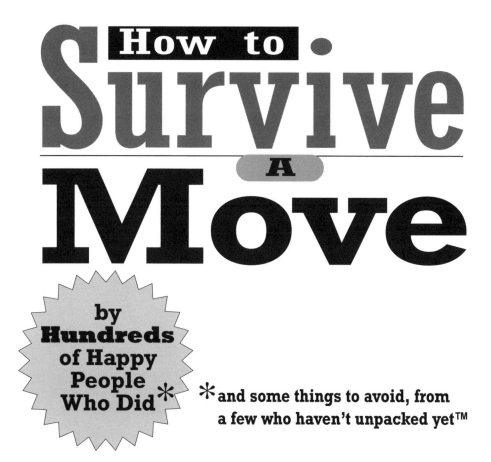

How to Survive a Move

by Hundreds of Happy People Who Did * *and some things to avoid, from a few who haven't unpacked yet™

edited by
JAMIE ALLEN AND KAZZ REGELMAN

Hundreds of Heads Books, Inc.
ATLANTA

Illustrations © 2005 by Image Club
See page 235 for credits and permissions.

Library of Congress Cataloging-in-Publication Data.
How to survive a move / by hundreds of happy people who did, and some things to avoid from a few who haven't unpacked yet; edited by Jamie Allen and Kazz Regelman.
     p. cm. -- (Hundreds of heads survival guide)
    ISBN 0-9746292-5-1
    1. Moving, Household--Anecdotes. 2. Homeowners--Interviews. I. Allen, Jamie 1968- II. Regelman, Kazz, 1968- III. Series.
    TX307.H68 2005
    648'.9--dc22

2004029881

Cover and book design by Elizabeth Johnsboen

Cover photograph by PictureQuest

HUNDREDS OF HEADS™ books are available at special discounts when purchased in bulk for premiums or institutional or educational use. Excerpts and custom editions can be created for specific uses. For more information, please email sales@hundredsofheads.com or write to:

HUNDREDS OF HEADS BOOKS, INC.
#230
2221 Peachtree Road, Suite D
Atlanta, GA 30309

ISBN 0-9746292-5-1

Printed in U.S.A.
10 9 8 7 6 5 4 3 2 1

6/06
BH

CONTENTS

Introduction

M oving is a unique experience for everyone. For some, it means tying a mattress to the roof of the car and driving down the block. For others, it's uprooting an entire family and relocating across the country or across the ocean. No matter how you do it, or when, it's always an adventure.

Now, movers everywhere should pack one more item on their trip: this book. Other advice books, no matter how smart or expert their authors, are generally limited to the knowledge of only one or two people. This book, the fifth in the HUNDREDS OF HEADS™ Survival Guide series, takes a different approach: We've talked to hundreds of people about their relocation experience and compiled their advice for your benefit. If two heads are better than one, as the saying goes, then we think hundreds of them are even better.

Among the words of wisdom collected here, you'll learn the best ways to pack your cat or dog (or, as the case may be, your fish). You'll be inspired to trash or sell half your stuff. You'll measure the benefits of professional movers vs. your willing, pizza-hungry friends. You'll help your kids with the tough transition. You'll find the perfect way to say goodbye to friends and family, and the best methods of packing and driving a giant truck. You'll learn fun ways to meet the new neighbors and get settled into your new home. And you'll experience, and hopefully learn from, our Worst Moves Ever.

You'll also realize that everyone has their own method for the madness of moving. When you interview this many people, not everyone agrees. For your benefit, we've put conflicting advice together. It's up to you to decide which approach works for you.

Best of all, in this book you'll read entertaining personal stories from people across the country—some funny, some inspiring, some downright practical. It's like inviting hundreds of your best friends to your house, sitting them down at the dinner table, and talking about the subjects that interest you.

So, read on. If life is an adventure, you're about to truly *live*. The road ahead might be fraught with peril, or paved with good times. Just remember to lift with your legs. Sooner or later, you'll get to where you're going. Our advice: Don't go it alone.

JAMIE ALLEN
KAZZ REGELMAN

KEY

So that you'll know just how expert our respondents really are, we've included their credentials in this book. Look for these icons:

     = 0-4 Moves
     = 5-7 Moves
     = 8 or more Moves

Making Your Move: Why Go, and Where?

*M*oving is one of the most challenging things you can do: Take your daily life and everything that's familiar, throw it all in the blender known as a moving truck, and see what comes out when you get to the other side. Yet it's precisely what 1 in every 7 Americans does every year. Why? Is it the adventure? The restlessness inherent in humans? Or, some sado-masochistic urge? And once you decide to move, how do you go about finding a good place to live? Your journey begins here.

I LIKE MOVING! It's an unknown adventure, into a better situation, just waiting for me to experience.

—*DENVER AQUINO*
LAS VEGAS, NEVADA
7 MOVES

MOVING IS THE MOST EXCITING THING YOU CAN DO.

—*SHARON LONDON*
SAN FRANCISCO, CALIFORNIA
5 MOVES

If there is a strong smell of deodorizer or potpourri, be suspicious.

—*CLINTON HAGER*
ROANOKE, VIRGINIA
6 MOVES

I DREAD THE ACTUAL PROCESS OF MOVING. I generally like relocating to a new space/neighborhood and the exploration and discovery that goes along with it, but when it comes to packing and hauling the stuff, I'll moan about it nonstop.

—*KRISTEN J. ELDE*
SEATTLE, WASHINGTON
10 MOVES

• • • • • • • •

WHEN LOOKING FOR AN APARTMENT, the phrase you should look for is "All utilities included."

—*DOMINIQUE COLEMAN*
SYRACUSE, NEW YORK
5 MOVES

• • • • • • • •

YOU HAVE TO MOVE FOR THE RIGHT REASONS. Moving for a job or a relationship can end in disaster. It's important to find a connection with the new environment for yourself. In the end, it won't be heavy boxes and a sore back that make the move miserable, but realizing that you made a mistake.

—*JOHN FRANCIS*
SAN DIEGO, CALIFORNIA
6 MOVES

• • • • • • • •

I'VE MOVED TO SIX COUNTRIES. Before each move we made a pro and con list. We included our children in the process. We added everything to the list—like missing friends, the chance to make more money, warm weather all year, changing schools, etc. Then we made the decision based on how many pros and how many cons we had. The pro side was always longer.

—*PAGET PERRAULT*
MELBOURNE, AUSTRALIA
6 MOVES

ENJOY NEW PLACES, because if you stay in one place too long you'll grow old quickly.

—*JOE SCHWAB*
DENVER, COLORADO

• • • • • • • •

" Go for it. Life is bigger than your comfortable little town, life or situation. Moving will help you realize how strong and self-sufficient you really are. "

—*CRISTOFFER L.*
SAN DIEGO, CALIFORNIA

• • • • • • • •

MOVING IS AN ADVENTURE—a chance to start over, meet new people, and see new places. It's a chance to set up a new house and make it your own, each time making changes and redefining yourself.

—*JENNIFER PIKE*
MONTICELLO, MINNESOTA
15 MOVES

• • • • • • • •

MOVING IS PURE HELL. It's as if a supreme being combined the worst elements of torture, scavenger hunts, paper cuts, and body fatigue into one painful, emotionally punishing episode. The only upside is that you are changing your life and getting into a new situation.

—*BART G. FARKAS*
COCHRANE, ALBERTA, CANADA
8 MOVES

WHEN ENOUGH IS ENOUGH

In the dead of winter, I was living in an apartment where the thermostat wasn't set right. It was 30 below outside and only 56 degrees inside. It was so cold that I'd put on long johns, sweatpants and a bathrobe, then lay in bed with the covers over me in a fetal position, shivering. I called my landlord to complain about 10 times. He didn't do anything except threaten to evict me if I complained again. I could have fought him, but instead I decided to find a new place when my lease was up. My landlord was not a nice guy. To stick around and battle it out with him would've made the problem much worse.

—JUDEE A.
MONTPELIER, VERMONT
20 MOVES

MAKE SURE YOU HAVE A GOOD, **REAL** REASON for moving—e.g. to be closer to family, move in with your fiancé, accept a great job or enter the witness protection program. Whether you move to Nowheresville or a fun, busy city, it helps to have a career to focus on or a relationship that provides you with support and a social outlet.

—*TINA MITRO*

IN ORDER TO MOVE JOYFULLY, you have to cultivate the feeling that you are "being moved," as if destiny has brought you right where you need to be.

—*MICHAEL ALPERSTEIN*
PETALUMA, CALIFORNIA
15 MOVES

MOVING IS A TIME TO CLARIFY really what is important to you. It's also a great opportunity to step out of your comfort zone, and reinvent yourself. Since moving, I've been exploring other things. I've had to meet new people, and all of a sudden I'm trying different things, which I don't think I'd have done if I'd stayed where I was.

—*M.Z. THWAITE WEEKS*
RIVERTON, NEW JERSEY
6 MOVES

LIVE NEAR YOUR FRIENDS. That way, you instantly know your neighbors. Every Saturday night, my friends and I ate chicken fajitas and hamburgers and played board games. I could go "out" by only moving 20 feet. It made me feel like part of a community and part of a family.

—*SHAWN W. HARWARD*
SAN ANTONIO, TEXAS
8 MOVES

If you rent your home, you are more than three times more likely to move in the next year than if you own.

—*MSN*

YOU KNOW IT'S TIME TO MOVE AGAIN when your family room can no longer accommodate your kids, their friends and the dog. They have all grown too big, and everything feels cramped and crowded.

—*ROBYN MURAMOTO*
CENTENNIAL, COLORADO
4 MOVES

Home sales peak in April, May and June. It is the prettiest time of year to sell and the weather is generally conducive to human comfort.

—*THE EVERYTHING HOMESELLING BOOK*

MAKE SURE YOU HAVE SOMEWHERE TO MOVE INTO after you're out of one place. We didn't plan it right, so my wife and I had to stay with my in-laws for six months in between houses. I don't wish that upon anyone.

—*C.S.*
IOWA CITY, IOWA
7 MOVES

YOUR NEW HOME SHOULD BE FAIRLY CLOSE to things like a gas station, supermarket and a restaurant. The first apartment my wife and I lived in was kind of isolated. One year there was a huge snowstorm and we couldn't get out of the house for a whole weekend. It would have been nice if there had been a market nearby. Instead, we ate pork and beans for three days.

—*MARTY L.*
EAST LIVERPOOL, OHIO
4 MOVES

WHEN LOOKING FOR A HOUSE, go with your instincts. After about a year of searching for a new home, my mother came across a small town where the school mascot is the hippo. She loves hippos and decided that she had found the place. She's been very happy there ever since, even though she is tempted to steal that school's hippo statue everyday.

—*DESIREÉ MARTINEZ*
SAN ANTONIO, TEXAS
5 MOVES

VIRTUAL HOME SHOPPING

The Internet can be a huge help in your search for a new abode. Here are some helpful hints about where to surf them out.

I FOUND MY LAST APARTMENT (in Seattle) by going to the classifieds at NWSource.com (http://classifieds.nwsource.com/rentals/). I found it easy to navigate to exactly which neighborhood interested me and to sort by price. They also keep them fairly up-to-date.

> —ANNETTE C. YOUNG
> VANCOUVER, WASHINGTON
> 8 MOVES

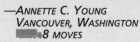

IF YOU'RE MOVING TO A BIG CITY, log onto Craigslist.org first—it's phenomenal. It's how I found a studio apartment, my roommates and two jobs when I moved to San Francisco. One word of warning, however: The helpfulness factor varies depending on the city you're moving to. In San Francisco, everybody uses Craigslist. In Denver, not so much.

> —LIBBY DEBLASIO
> DENVER, COLORADO
> 7 MOVES

THE LAST TIME WE MOVED, we used Yahoo for maps, and my wife checked out the city online, browsing the online version of the newspaper and looking at rental listings. Given how much information is available online these days, the Internet can often give you a very good idea of what to expect in your new location.

> —BRAD COOK
> CHICO, CALIFORNIA
> 6 MOVES

TAKE MY ADVICE—never go to look at a potential house at night. In the dusk of a late September evening, the rustic 200-year-old farmhouse I'd rented in Brewster, New York seemed to have everything I was looking for. But the previous night's rain had created axle-breaking potholes in the road, turning it into a deadly carnival ride. Pulling into my parking space, I watched my spotless classic car slowly sink in the mud.

—MICHAEL JEFFERSON
MOUNT KISCO, NEW YORK
4 MOVES

• • • • • • • •

" When I was a kid my family moved across the street and five houses down. Never do this. It was the most frustrating and futile packing process ever. "

—ISABELLA
CHAMPAIGN, ILLINOIS

• • • • • • • •

CHECK OUT THE CARS IN THE NEIGHBORHOOD you are considering. Make sure that they all have tires on them, that the windows are not knocked out and covered with plastic and that they have no big locks on the steering wheel.

—K.S.
BALTIMORE, MARYLAND
8 MOVES

RESEARCH THE NEW HOMETOWN EXTENSIVELY on the Internet and watch the real estate market online. Consider it a new adventure after asking, "Do we really need to go?"

—*SHARLANE BLAISE*
PORTLAND, OREGON
🚚 *1 MOVE*

• • • • • • • •

DO NOT MOVE INTO A FOURTH-FLOOR WALK-UP apartment with your girlfriend. You'll end up carrying everything up and down the stairs, including the laundry.

—*J.P.*
NEW YORK, NEW YORK
🚚 *8 MOVES*

• • • • • • • •

EVEN IF LIVING QUARTERS ARE HARD TO FIND, don't allow yourself to take a place too far from where you work. When I moved to New York City, I wound up in an apartment in Jamaica, Queens. By subway, it was 1 hour and 45 minutes to work. And I had 3 jobs! I was a mess; I was never home. I would finish work at 1 or 2 in the morning, then I had to take the train all the way back. As soon as possible, I moved closer.

—*BRANDON CUTRELL*
COLUMBUS, INDIANA

• • • • • • • •

YOU NEVER KNOW WHEN YOU'LL FIND your dream place. A few months ago I was looking in the newspaper and saw a tiny classified ad for an apartment. It didn't sound like anything special, but the next day, I went to look at it, fell in love, and signed the lease on the spot!

—*SHARON NAYLOR*
MADISON, NEW JERSEY
🚚 *10 MOVES*

Nearly 45 percent of all moves occur between Memorial Day and Labor Day.

—*U-HAUL*

THINK ABOUT HOW YOU LIKE TO SPEND YOUR TIME, and pick a place where it's convenient to do those things. I teach yoga, so I made sure to be close to some studios where I could teach. Tranquility is important to me, so we're near a park. No matter how much you like a house, if you don't like the neighborhood, or if you find yourself commuting all the time to everything, you'll be miserable.

—*E.*
SAN FRANCISCO, CALIFORNIA
3 MOVES

• • • • • • • •

DO YOUR RESEARCH. Visit the place you may move to and do things like go to a grocery store, go out to dinner, go to the mall and drive around the neighborhood. That way, you get to see how people interact with you and each other.

—*GABRYELA COMPEAN*
RIO MEDINA, TEXAS
3 MOVES

• • • • • • • •

WHILE INVESTIGATING A NEIGHBORHOOD or a particular building, ask the locals for their opinion. At an apartment building I was interested in, I pushed buttons until I found someone home. The guy who answered let me up into the building and answered all my questions about neighbors, rodents, and utilities. You can also ask people on the street. I stopped a woman and asked her if it was a safe area. She gave me good information. People usually tend to be helpful, and want to show what they know.

—*AMANDA SLAUGHTER*
BUFFALO, NEW YORK

Best cities for singles: Boston, Austin, Washington DC-Baltimore, Raleigh-Durham, Denver-Boulder.

—*FORBES*

I HAD ONLY ONE CRITERION: I just wanted a dishwasher. I'd been washing dishes by hand for 5 years, and was ready for a change.

—*JEREMY FORCÉ*
NARRAGANSETT, RHODE ISLAND
12 MOVES

" Avoid living near lots of boys between the ages of 14 and 19. They love loud music, hang out in groups of 8, drink, rev their cars, and drive dangerously. They all should be exiled to an island. "

—*S.C.*
SAN ANTONIO, TEXAS
40 MOVES

WHEN I MOVE, I look for parks and neighborhoods with kids. Good school districts, sports leagues, and community centers are important for families.

—*D.L.*
CHICAGO, ILLINOIS
8 MOVES

EARLY ON, WE DECIDED WHAT MATTERED MOST to us for our new home: a neighborhood with kids, dogs, and a good hospital nearby. Identifying these criteria early really helped to narrow our search.

—*SANDI*
ALLENTOWN, PENNSYLVANIA
1 MOVE

SELL YOURSELVES . . .

When we first moved to Los Angeles 5 years ago we got really discouraged while trying to buy a house. The market is crazy and when we finally found a house that we loved and was in our price-range, they already had 3 other bids in place. The original owners called us and said we didn't get the house because another couple had put 50% down. From there I just went into sell mode because really, both my husband and I had great jobs, were getting paid well, had been pre-approved for our loans—so why should it matter whether we put 50% down or 5% down?

I called the owner and pleaded our case. The other couple was just buying the house for investment purposes—they never planned to live there. We really wanted to raise a family in that house and we wanted our baby to have a great backyard like that in Los Angeles. Then I reiterated how we weren't a risk—both employed with great jobs, no problems getting approved for loans, etc. By the morning we got a call from the owner saying she had reconsidered and wanted us to have it! We couldn't believe it. Do not give up on a house you really want!

—M. SOELBERG
LOS ANGELES, CALIFORNIA
5 MOVES

IF POSSIBLE, GIVE YOURSELF PLENTY OF TIME to check out the place you're moving to. When I moved to Chicago, I had to start my new job right away and needed a place to live in immediately. I moved into an apartment that, in retrospect, didn't meet my needs. Three months later, I found a place that worked better for me, so I moved again. If I had had more time to look to begin with, I might have found a better fit from the start.

—*ROBERT MUCHA*
CHICAGO, ILLINOIS
5 MOVES

• • • • • • • •

SIT IN THE POTENTIAL APARTMENT AND LISTEN to see how loud the outside noise is. A quick walk through the new apartment won't measure how thin your walls/windows are! I wish I had done that before signing the lease at my new place. I hear their every whisper and got in trouble recently for cheering during a Yankee game.

—*BRIAN R.*
NEW YORK, NEW YORK
2 MOVES

• • • • • • • •

IF YOU'RE MOVING TO AN UNFAMILIAR CITY and you're trying to find a good neighborhood or apartment to live in, pay attention to the kinds of cars that are parked in the area. Do the cars look well maintained, or do they look visibly in need of repair? If the people who live there don't take good care of their cars, they probably don't take good care of their residence.

—*M.B.*
EDMOND, OKLAHOMA
3 MOVES

Consider cost of living: You need to earn almost $57,000 in San Francisco to match the buying power of the $27,000 you earn in Birmingham, Alabama.

—*CNN.COM*

LOOK IN THE RESTAURANT GUIDES for the kinds of places that you like to go—not fancy once-in-a-while places but regular places for when you just don't feel like cooking. Those are the neighborhoods to check out.

—*DANI*
  SAN FRANCISCO, CALIFORNIA
  10 MOVES

• • • • • • • •

Don't live next door to a liquor store with bulletproof glass that sells '40s' and wine with screw tops.

—*K.S.*
  BALTIMORE, MARYLAND
  8 MOVES

• • • • • • • •

I'M ITALIAN, SO WHEN I MOVED TO TOWN I knew I would like the Italian neighborhood. My landlord was Italian. My neighbors were Italian. There were Italian restaurants and bakeries nearby, and I could walk to work. It felt like a real home.

—*JASON*
  MYSTIC, CONNECTICUT
  3 MOVES

• • • • • • • •

IF YOU'RE LOOKING AT HOUSES and find one you really love, don't keep looking. If the house is what you want and the price is right, chances are you'll never find one like that again. It's not like shopping for clothes.

—*ROSETTA HAMMOND*
  LOUISVILLE, KENTUCKY

FIND A PLACE WITH THICK WALLS if you don't want to hear other people's business. We rented one apartment where we could hear the couple above us having sex. Every time they came home we'd hear them climbing the steps and then, minutes later, we could hear them going at it right above our bedroom. Most times it was funny but some nights it was just annoying.

>   —*ANGELA*
>   *FROSTBURG, MARYLAND*
>   *3 MOVES*

* * * * * * * *

HAVING A PLACE TO MOVE TO when the time comes to move out of your current residence is always a good tip—one I should have followed when I moved last fall. I ended up sleeping on my mattress at a friend's house in the middle of the hall for two weeks. It was no fun at all.

>   —*HEATHER S.*
>   *PACIFIC BEACH, CALIFORNIA*
>   *7 MOVES*

* * * * * * * *

IN EXTREMELY COMPETITIVE HOUSING MARKETS, you must bid above the asking price. Houses can go in one day, so to make the offer attractive you have to have your bid in on time. Another thing that helped us was writing a personal letter with a photo of us—happy newlyweds—telling the owners that it would be our first house together and explaining why the house was perfect for us, how much we loved the neighborhood, etc. In another market, they might have laughed at us for doing that, but in our case, it sealed the deal!

>   —*LINDSEY GAWRON CALDWELL*
>   *ARLINGTON, VIRGINIA*
>   *1 MOVE*

Move every two years. Otherwise, the dust bunnies never get cleaned.

>   —*SHANON DRAYTON*
>   *LOS ANGELES,*
>   *CALIFORNIA*
>   *30 MOVES*

WHEN CHOOSING A HOME, consider how far away you are from a police station and how long the response time will be if you should need to call them.

—ANA VIGIL
OLMOS PARK, TEXAS
 1 MOVE

· · · · · · · ·

SOME SAY NOT TO LIVE IN THE SAME BUILDING as your landlords, but I had a good experience. Mine were a nice family from Italy. They had a small plot of land that they used to cultivate peaches and eggplants and beefsteak tomatoes. I would often come home and find a bag of something waiting for me on the doorknob.

—GIDEON D'ARCANGELO
BROOKLYN, NEW YORK
12 MOVES

· · · · · · · ·

IF YOU ARE OBSESSIVE, moving gives you a great opportunity to clean your things before you pack them, and then again after you unpack.

—SHARON LONDON
SAN FRANCISCO, CALIFORNIA
5 MOVES

· · · · · · · ·

ALWAYS CHECK THE WATER PRESSURE. You don't want a shower that drips at its full potential. Also, make sure the temperature doesn't go from hot to cold at random so you scald and then freeze yourself in the shower and have to fumble with the temperature knobs while soap is burning your eyes out.

—PEGGY
VANCOUVER, BRITISH COLUMBIA, CANADA

Make sure you are not commuting with the masses.

—K.S.
BALTIMORE, MARYLAND
8 MOVES

BUY NEWSPAPERS FROM YOUR NEW TOWN to help you get acquainted. Don't be afraid to ask lots of questions to real estate people, lawyers, even future neighbors. You need to know about schools, places of worship, shopping possibilities, the post office, doctors, utility companies, banks, and fun things for kids to do.

> —*ROBERTA BEACH JACOBSON*
> *KARPATHOS, GREECE*
> *8 MOVES*

* * * * * * * *

"If the description says 'lots of potential,' it's a dead giveaway that it needs some serious work. Avoid it, unless you specifically want a fixer-upper and are a glutton for punishment."

> —*SEAN H.*
> *NEW YORK, NEW YORK*
> *12 MOVES*

* * * * * * * *

NEVER BUY A PLACE RIGHT AWAY, even if you have the money. Rent first in a neighborhood you think you'll like and do a lot of exploring in other neighborhoods as well. It takes at least a couple of months to get the feel of a new city. I rushed into a neighborhood I thought was perfect for me only to turn around and sell the house less than two years later. What a hassle!

> —*STEPH D.*
> *BALTIMORE, MARYLAND*
> *4 MOVES*

Moving is great because you can start fresh and become the person you want to be. It's a clean slate.

—MELISSA WILLIAMS
MANHATTAN
BEACH, CALIFORNIA
3 MOVES

CALL THE CHAMBER OF COMMERCE in the state you are moving to for information on the economy, school systems, healthcare, etc. They will send out extensive information to your home before your move.

—ANONYMOUS
BIRMINGHAM, ALABAMA
6 MOVES

• • • • • • • •

MY PARENTS ALWAYS TOLD ME: the best thing to do in a new locale is to rent for a year. Although I really enjoy having a place of my own, renting for a year allowed me to make a lot of progress in creating new friendships, finding the right places to shop, etc. Ultimately, this gave me a great feel for where I would want to buy a house.

—DON DASHER
SARATOGA, CALIFORNIA
10 MOVES

• • • • • • • •

LIVE EAST OF WHERE YOU WORK. That way, your commute does not involve driving with the sun in your eyes.

—CHRISTINE C. GODIN
SAN ANTONIO, TEXAS
12 MOVES

• • • • • • • •

IT'S WORTH SPENDING A FEW HUNDRED BUCKS to have a knowledgeable contractor walk through any house you're serious about buying with you. We took a contractor through three houses. Yes, it cost us about $1,000. But we saved much, much more than that by NOT buying the first or second houses, both of which had major problems that we would never have seen on our own.

—K. JONES
PHILADELPHIA, PENNSYLVANIA
8 MOVES

KEEP YOUR EYES OPEN. When my husband and I were searching for our first house, finding an area that had good schools was a top priority, so we paid close attention to the yards in every neighborhood. We were looking for basketball hoops, Little Tikes plastic toys, bicycles—any indication that lots of happy children lived nearby.

> —*ROBYN MURAMOTO*
> *CENTENNIAL, COLORADO*
> *4 MOVES*

• • • • • • • •

CHECK TO SEE HOW MANY OUTLETS THERE ARE before committing to a place. I didn't realize until after the fact that there was only one outlet for my entire apartment. By this point, I'd already moved in, paid my first and last months' rent, as well as a security deposit. I was forced to run extension cords everywhere. By the time I moved out a year later, you'd best believe I'd learned my lesson.

> —*E.C.*
> *NEW YORK, NEW YORK*
> *15 MOVES*

• • • • • • • •

BEFORE I BOUGHT MY PLACE, I drove by it one night, walked around the area, and asked a neighbor I ran into what it was truly like to live in the area. His response? "Really quiet," which has generally turned out to be true. There's nothing more accurate than first-hand information. Actively seek it out.

> —*LEITH WALDROP*
> *TULSA, OKLAHOMA*
> *2 MOVES*

Make a list of your favorite activities and give it to your real estate agent. He or she should get back to you with a list of places that cater to these activities.

—*The Unofficial Guide to Buying a Home*

BUY A PLACE THAT YOU'RE GOING TO BE super psyched about coming home to every night. I used to travel a lot for business and the cab ride to the airport always took me past this gorgeous building in Chicago. Every time I'd go past, I'd think, "I'm going to buy a place there someday." So, six years later, when I had saved enough for a down payment, I didn't get a broker or realtor. I just went to the building and found a condo for sale and bought it. I couldn't be happier.

— *Kent M. Zimmermann*
Chicago, Illinois
🚚 *6 MOVES*

· · · · · · · ·

MY PHILOSOPHY ABOUT FINDING a good place is that all you need in life is your donkey and a view. Your donkey is the freedom you have to move around and take vacations, and the view makes you feel happy when you have a quiet day at home. My fiancé and I looked at a beautiful and very big house—but it overlooked the freeway—and I knew I couldn't live there because a nice or peaceful view is too important for me to pass up.

— *Lahna*
Los Angeles, California
🚚 *7 MOVES*

Where to Begin? Planning Your Move

C ongratulations! That new place you found is perfect for you. Your life will begin anew . . . once you move all your stuff from one house to the next. When you start to plan your move, figuring out what to do first can be more than a little daunting. There are countless details to consider. Before you start to panic, take a deep breath . . . we're here to help! Here's some advice on how to put one foot in front of the other, and get yourself out the door— eventually.

LIKE ALL BIG THINGS IN LIFE, break the moving process down into little pieces. Keep this little saying in mind: "Inch by inch, it's a cinch. Yard by yard, it's very hard."

—*RUTH DRESCHER*
PITTSBURGH, PENNSYLVANIA
4 MOVES

GET EVERYTHING IN WRITING!

—*MONIKA*
TORONTO, ONTARIO, CANADA
7 MOVES

PLAN YOUR MOVES LIKE YOU WOULD A WEDDING: with a to-do checklist, broken down by time period. Three months ahead of time, clean your house and donate anything you don't want or need to charity. A month prior, research the area you're moving to, get a change-of-address form from the post office and gather boxes. A week before, start packing everything except essential clothing, toiletries and food. A few days before, eat the leftover food in your refrigerator and turn on the utilities in your new house. Breaking tasks down like this is essential because it keeps you organized and helps you remember the important things.

> —*L.K.*
> *NASHVILLE, TENNESSEE*
> *8 MOVES*

• • • • • • • • •

MAKE A TIME-LINE OF EVENTS IN THE PROCESS to the finest detail. Make a list of address changes before leaving. Open a new bank account early. Organize your important papers in file folders. List important transfers: insurance, drivers license, medical. If moving out of state, get contacts early (i.e. utilities, medical, insurance contacts).

> —*SHARLANE BLAISE*
> *PORTLAND, OREGON*
> *1 MOVE*

• • • • • • • • •

DO NOT FORWARD MAIL—just tell important people/contacts that you're somewhere new. It's a good way to avoid all the junk mail and solicitations that have accumulated over the years. Now that I think about it, everybody should move often for this reason alone!

> —*AL*
> *TORONTO, ONTARIO, CANADA*
> *6 MOVES*

If you live in an old home, prepare a brief history of the structure—construction dates, materials used, changes over the years, and residents who lived there.

—*THE EVERYTHING HOMESELLING BOOK*

START PREPARING NOW. No matter how far you're going, moving is a big deal. I've been sorting through my things, organizing, donating, and throwing things out. It's taking a long time, but I'm determined that by the time I'm ready to move, all of my belongings should fit in my Honda Civic!

—*JUDY BECK*
   PERKASIE, PENNSYLVANIA
   2 MOVES

" I know a lot of people say you shouldn't move when you're pregnant, but the nice thing is that no one—not even the movers—lets you do anything. You just get to sit around and direct traffic. "

—*KRISTIN SWEETSER*
   REDMOND, WASHINGTON
   8 MOVES

YOU MUST CHECK OUT THE SCHOOLS before you decide on a place to live. Don't rely on the appearance of the neighborhood. We once moved into a really nice neighborhood but it turned out we were on the wrong side of the street to be in the good school district. My daughter had to go to a really scary school for a couple of months before we were able to get her in somewhere else.

—*J.G.*
   CHAPEL HILL, NORTH CAROLINA
   5 MOVES

Exercise for 2 months before you move because it takes a toll on your body. It's good to be in good shape for an endeavor like this.

—*RICK*
  LOS ANGELES,
  CALIFORNIA
  6 MOVES

DON'T SCHEDULE A MOVE AROUND YOUR DUE DATE. When I got pregnant with our second child, we decided our house was too small and started looking to move. We found a great house, but the timing meant we'd be closing right at the time my son was due. We packed a lot before he was born, but ended up moving truckloads over the course of a couple weeks after he was born. It would have been much, much easier if we had allowed more time or scheduled the closing better.

—*ANDREA COX*
  GRAND LAKE, COLORADO
  4 MOVES

• • • • • • • •

DON'T FORGET TO FORWARD YOUR MAIL, even if the house you're leaving is still yours, even if you keep visiting it to pick up the occasional thing (including the mail). We showed up at our old house before it sold, and the mailbox was tied shut with a rubber band. We found out that the postal service did it—they don't deliver anything to houses where people are no longer living, even if you still stop by to pick up the mail.

—*JWAIII*
  ATLANTA, GEORGIA
  15 MOVES

• • • • • • • •

WHEN YOU'RE MOVING, realize you may need to eat out quite a lot during the time you are packing and moving, and put aside some extra money (if you have any left) for that extra expense. When dishes, silverware, and food are being packed and moved—and grocery shopping comes to a screeching halt—getting Chinese takeout is a good option amid all the chaos.

—*STEVE*
  ALLENTOWN, PENNSYLVANIA
  1 MOVE

BE SURE TO CALL FOR A MOVING VAN at least two months in advance during high season (summer) because the rental companies will take your reservation and if they don't have a truck to give you, you're out of luck. It's usually first come, first serve. If you don't have to put down a deposit, I would make as many reservations as you can with other local rental agencies.

—*G.P.*
IOWA CITY, IOWA
5 MOVES

• • • • • • • •

FIND GOOD MOVERS. They're like mechanics— honest ones are hard to find and they book up quickly, especially if you're moving out on the first of the month.

—*TED*
TORONTO, ONTARIO, CANADA
5 MOVES

• • • • • • • •

CONTACT YOUR PHONE COMPANY AND ISP at least a month in advance with your new information. I gave them only a couple weeks last time and they royally messed things up. If I'd had some buffer time, I would have been golden when I arrived.

—*ANNETTE C. YOUNG*
VANCOUVER, WASHINGTON
8 MOVES

• • • • • • • •

SET ASIDE AT LEAST YOUR CURRENT MONTH'S RENT for the move: Between renting a truck, paying for gas, turning utilities on at your new place and ordering take-out every day, your money will get eaten up fast!

—*DAWN COLCLASURE-WILSON*
RANCHO MIRAGE, CALIFORNIA
4 MOVES

Three important moving tips: Plan ahead. Make your reservations as far in advance as possible. Try moving on a weekday, when banks, utilities and government offices are open.

—*U-HAUL*

There are more than 800,000 address changes in America each week.

—ABOUT.COM

MAKE LISTS EARLY. Several weeks before you move, write down all of the places that will need your change of address and list the utilities that you need to turn off at the old place, and on at the new place.

> *—MICHAEL REICH*
> *HELLERTOWN, PENNSYLVANIA*
> 🚚 *4 MOVES*

• • • • • • • •

IT SOUNDS STUPID, but you need to pay all of your parking tickets in your old city before leaving for a new one. It's something that most people forget to do, but once you leave, it's harder to track down what you owe. I knew that I owed about $40 after I moved, but when I called to pay by phone, the lady on the other end said I owed $75. It wasn't worth it to argue, but I could have had I been there in person.

> *—M.S.*
> *EVANSTON, ILLINOIS*
> 🚚 *3 MOVES*

MONEY, AND MORE MONEY

Make sure you have a good cushion of cash available—at least 6 months' worth of expenses. When I moved to San Diego 2 years ago, I had $5,000 with me, which I thought would be plenty. However, between rent, deposit, gas to get out there and way too many meals out, I blew through that in about 2 months. To make matters worse, the job I'd originally lined up didn't pan out and I couldn't find work. I finally had to e-mail my friends back home, who were nice enough to gather together and send me a check for $1,000.

> *—STEVE DECESS*
> *HIGHLANDS RANCH, COLORADO*
> 🚚 *7 MOVES*

ALWAYS HAVE YOUR CAR CHECKED for maintenance before moving. I traveled from Ann Arbor, Michigan to Iowa City this summer and the whole time I had a loose and eroded front wheel bearing. When I finally took it in to get an oil change, the mechanic told me I was lucky that I didn't lose the wheel on the road!

—*MICHAEL STENERSON*
DULUTH, MINNESOTA
10 MOVES

" Change your address for bills. There's nothing more annoying than having to track down bills from your old landlord or the new person living at your place. And lost bills will cost you money in late payments. "

—*TED*
TORONTO, ONTARIO, CANADA
5 MOVES

I START PACKING THINGS like craft supplies, out-of-season clothes and extra linen about six months early. I suggest stacking boxes away with a written note on the front side telling what is inside each box. This is helpful when sorting boxes and unpacking at your new house as well.

—*MALAY THAO*
STOW, OHIO
2 MOVES

THINK ABOUT ALL YOUR FINANCES. I was awake the whole night before I finally moved into my own apartment for the first time, worrying about affording everything.

—*H.L.*
WILMINGTON, DELAWARE
🚚 *5 MOVES*

• • • • • • • •

WHEN YOU MOVE, you'll likely receive free address labels in the mail from nonprofit organizations. Be sure to check that the information is correct! I used a bunch of these address labels for weeks before I noticed that my last name was misspelled "Ruch."

—*JENNIFER BRIGHT REICH*
HELLERTOWN, PENNSYLVANIA
🚚 *6 MOVES*

• • • • • • • •

❝ Take a detailed inventory of everything that's broken or damaged AND clean your apartment before you move out. ❞

—*SUSAN*
WESTFIELD, NEW JERSEY
🚚 *5 MOVES*

• • • • • • • •

HIRE PROFESSIONAL CLEANERS BEFORE YOU MOVE out of an apartment. You don't want to give your landlord any legal reason to hold onto your security deposit.

—*T.M.*
PITTSBURGH, PENNSYLVANIA
🚚 *3 MOVES*

DON'T FORGET TO BACK UP YOUR ADDRESSES and anything else from your computer on a disk. Our computer got damaged in the move, and we were just going to throw it away and get a new one, since it was pretty old. But then we realized it had all of our contacts on it, and we didn't know how to track down some of those people otherwise. We ended up paying a technician over a hundred bucks to retrieve the information from our damaged old computer.

> —J.D.
> BALTIMORE, MARYLAND
> 2 MOVES

THE HARDEST PART OF MOVING TO EUROPE: the paperwork. Since all the documents were in either French or Flemish, we didn't understand what we were signing. And we made all the mistakes in the book: filled out the wrong forms incorrectly, submitted them late, etc. The next time, we'll get a relocation company!

> —MEREDITH E.
> FAIRFIELD, CONNECTICUT
> MOVED TO EUROPE

IF IT'S POSSIBLE, GIVE YOURSELF PLENTY OF TIME to move. I'd even go so far as to pay for an extra month's rent or mortgage. My husband and I had a month to move from our apartment into our first home. It was great to have such a luxurious amount of time. We moved one room at a time. First we cleaned our bedroom in our new house, then painted it, then moved the furniture over, and then we moved on to the next room. Because we had so much time, we were able to completely repaint the new house before we moved in.

> —DEANNA
> MACUNGIE, PENNSYLVANIA
> 3 MOVES

Call your local U.S. Department of Agriculture office to see if your plants are restricted in your new state—some might harbor bugs or pests that can destroy valuable crops.
—HOMEDEPOT
MOVING.COM

Whatever the estimate for the price of your move, double it.

—*Sasha Emmons*
Brooklyn,
New York
7 moves

Moving is moving, whether it's across the street or across the country. Sometimes when I've moved a short distance, I wasn't careful packing. I broke dishes and dropped things because I tried to carry them by hand. Plus, it took about 5 times as long to move because I didn't take the time to pack things in boxes. It doesn't matter how far you're moving; take the time to do it right.

—*Ellen*
Pittsburgh, Pennsylvania
11 moves

• • • • • • • •

Be careful when you shut off the utilities. The last time we moved we shut the power off in the old place before we'd cleaned it, not realizing we would need power to do so. We rented a steam cleaner so we had to plug it into someone else's apartment.

—*Nicole Moran*
Groveland, Massachusetts
5 moves

• • • • • • • •

Set up a free Hotmail or Yahoo e-mail account before you move if your regular e-mail account is tied to your phone or is through a local provider. E-mail all your contacts (friends and family) with your new home address and phone number and tell them to contact you until further notice at the Hotmail account. Then when you get a new account set up, make sure you e-mail everybody right away and give them your new address. Keep checking Hotmail for a while in case there are stragglers.

—*Rachel B.*
Philadelphia, Pennsylvania
5 moves

THE POOR GIRL'S GUIDE TO MOVING

1) PLAN AHEAD. Make lists of tasks and deadlines, and post them.

2) SEPARATE YOUR POSSESSIONS INTO 2 CATEGORIES: things you can't live without and things you might be able to sell.

3) START PACKING IMMEDIATELY. You have twice as much stuff as you realize.

4) EVERY SINGLE TIME YOU LEAVE YOUR APARTMENT, take something out the door with you.

5) EVERY TIME SOMEONE ELSE LEAVES YOUR APARTMENT, they must have something of yours in their hands.

6) PAY THE AIRLINE TO TAKE EXTRA SUITCASES. You can cram a lot into a suitcase, and it costs much less than shipping.

7) GIVE YOUR FRIENDS PACKED SUITCASES TO BRING with them when they come to visit.

8) KEEP YOUR HOUSE STOCKED WITH READY-MADE FOOD: salad kits, deli slices, etc. It's easy to spend a fortune eating out when you are in the process of moving.

9) TRY TO FINISH YOUR PACKING AND CLEANING EARLY. Don't put yourself in the position of staying up late, night after night, the week before your move.

10) IF YOU'VE BEEN LIVING IN ANOTHER COUNTRY, buy some mementos and take them with you to your new home.

—HESTER KAMIN

WHEN I MOVED OUT OF MY APARTMENT I figured my carpet was clean enough to pass the inspection. It turns out that I got a bill at my new address for more than $200. If you're thinking of skipping the professional carpet cleaning, pay the $50 to rent a machine and don't blow it off.

—BOB
CHICAGO, ILLINOIS
2 MOVES

• • • • • • • •

" When moving, go to the post office to arrange mail forwarding. It's worth every penny and every minute of your time. You'll always forget to contact and update somebody important! "

—JANNA HAROWITZ
TORONTO, ONTARIO, CANADA
6 MOVES

• • • • • • • •

DON'T BE AFRAID TO ASK IF YOU CAN MOVE things into a garage or shed before your actual moving day. My husband and I did this when we moved into our home, and the former owners let us move our things into the garage two weeks before. This was so incredibly helpful because we could bring things over a little at a time. It made moving day much easier.

—MOLLY BROWN
ALLENTOWN, PENNSYLVANIA
4 MOVES

Boxed In: Packing Tips

*S*cissors? Check. Tape? Check. Boxes? Check. Bubble wrap? Check. Willingness to stay up late at night going through all your items, carefully wrapping them and placing them in boxes? A month of extra time to make sure it all gets done the right way? Hmmm . . . Everyone has a method to the madness of packing. Check out these tips before you get started on yours.

I USE SOCKS TO PACK MY GLASSWARE. It cushions the glass, and then I have one less thing to pack.

—*JOELLE SELLNER*
LOS ANGELES, CALIFORNIA
8 MOVES

DON'T OVERLOAD BOXES, ESPECIALLY WITH BOOKS.

—*L.A.*
IOWA CITY, IOWA
4 MOVES

I LOVE MOVING. I love the catharsis that comes with cleaning out closets and ridding myself of useless possessions. I love the adventure of a new place, the creativity in organizing and decorating a new abode. I love moving—except for the actual packing and hauling part.

　　　—*ALYSSA AGEE*
　　　　SNOQUALMIE, WASHINGTON
　　　　■10 MOVES

• • • • • • • •

MAKE A LIST OF WHAT YOU TAKE. As I was packing up my stuff for school, I made a huge list of everything that I was taking. I also included details like the serial number from my computer, in case it is ever stolen. As I packed things, I checked them off of my list, to make sure I wasn't forgetting anything. I'll use this list again when I pack up my things in spring to move home, to make sure nothing is left behind.

　　　—*BRANDI SMITH*
　　　　DUBOIS, PENNSYLVANIA
　　　　■ 1 MOVE

• • • • • • • •

Leave everything behind and go to IKEA!

—*JAN SIMMONDS*
NEW YORK,
NEW YORK
■ 2 MOVES

TRASH BAGS ARE A HUGE HELP. You can throw anything into them: clothes, stuffed animals, books.

　　　—*DAWN COLCLASURE-WILSON*
　　　　RANCHO MIRAGE, CALIFORNIA
　　　　■ 4 MOVES

• • • • • • • •

GET A VARIETY OF SIZES OF ZIPLOC BAGGIES and a Sharpie marker. Whenever you take apart a piece of furniture, put all of the nuts and bolts into one of the baggies and label it clearly. This prevents important pieces from getting lost.

　　　—*STACEY MCHARGUE*
　　　　SAN ANTONIO, TEXAS
　　　　■10 MOVES

To find boxes, I made trips to the liquor store, since their boxes are a size a normal person can carry, and many beer boxes have cut-out handles. Also, they have boxes divided into 24 slots (great for glasses) and 4 slots (great for cookie jars, canisters, small appliances). I called first to see which day and time was best to pick up boxes, since I did not want to be a pest.

—*Jill Marie Davis*
Weehawken, New Jersey
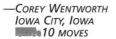 *12 moves*

. . . .

" French fry boxes from fast food restaurants are the best to pack with. Call in the morning and they will save some for you to pick up later. They are sturdy and a perfect square shape. "

—*Corey Wentworth*
Iowa City, Iowa
10 moves

. . . .

Keep all the original appliance boxes for moves—especially for your computer and monitor. I didn't. I was so nervous when I packed them in other boxes; I was sure they would arrive in lots of small pieces. But I wrapped them in pillows and towels. And I said a few prayers! They arrived in perfect condition. Next time, I'll just keep the boxes!

—*Aida S.*
New Orleans, Louisiana
1 time (to Europe)

LABEL WITH CARE

WHEN WE MOVED INTO A NEW HOUSE IN HIGH SCHOOL, I packed all of my sports trophies and medals in one box and labeled it "Trophies Mike's Room." It even had gold medals I'd won from the Maccabi games in there. When we got to the new place, everything was there except that box—the movers had stolen it and there was nothing I could do. Don't label a box with what's inside if it's something important. Now, all I have are pictures from my sports experiences as a child.

—*MIKE*
CHICAGO, ILLINOIS
*8 MOVES*

. . . .

LABEL EACH BOX WITH A LETTER indicating how important the items inside are. For example, I write "A" on boxes with things that are very important and will need to be unpacked right away, such as silverware. I write "B" on boxes filled with items that aren't so critical, which my family could get along without for a few days. And I write "C" on boxes that are the last to be put away.

—*ED REICH*
DUBOIS, PENNSYLVANIA
4 MOVES

. . . .

DECIDE AHEAD OF TIME where your things will go in your new abode. Label your boxes accordingly. Always have a shoebox or other container labeled VIP, "Very Important Papers." Right now, my passport is hiding in an unknown box, most likely in storage.

—*MINDY PHILLIPS LAWRENCE*
FARMINGTON, MISSOURI
8 MOVES

UPS HAS THESE REALLY COOL clear plastic sleeve covers that you can order for free from their website; they make labeling moving boxes so much easier! Simply attach one of the sleeve covers to the outside of a box, write on a separate sheet of paper exactly what that box contains, and slip the paper inside the sleeve cover. The beauty of this system is you never have to ruin your original boxes by writing on them, so you can use them over and over again.

> —*CARRIE K.*
> *CHICAGO, ILLINOIS*
> *5 MOVES*

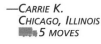

CARDBOARD BOXES ARE ANNOYING—they're hard to find and will look dirty in your new and clean place. Buy some nice containers that you can use again, in case you don't want to unpack everything but still want to feel organized.

> —*ALEX*
> *TORONTO, ONTARIO, CANADA*
> *6 MOVES*

BIG BOXES SEEM LIKE A REALLY GREAT IDEA when you're packing, because they hold more and you need less of them. But then you're carrying a big computer monitor box of kitchen stuff up the stairs at your new place, and you remember that smaller ones weigh less.

> —*MIKE EMERY*
> *UPPER ARLINGTON, OHIO*
> *3 MOVES*

USE PLASTIC GROCERY BAGS, dish towels and clothes to wrap breakables. Then you won't have to deal with all that newspaper.

> —*L.O.*
> *SYRACUSE, NEW YORK*
> *5 MOVES*

I pull an all-nighter the night before I have to move and throw everything in a box.

> —*G.P.*
> *IOWA CITY, IOWA*
> *5 MOVES*

I SUPPOSE ONE SHOULD HANDLE BREAKABLES with care, using the appropriate packing materials (peanuts, tissue, newspaper, etc.) to ensure the intact arrival of items. However, I seem to lose patience after about 10 minutes, at which point I resort to creatively wedging coffee mugs and dinner plates between layers of clothing and bath towels and just hoping for the best.

—*KRISTEN J. ELDE*
SEATTLE, WASHINGTON
10 MOVES

. . . .

" I discovered an endless supply of boxes at the local recycling center. I just borrow the boxes and return them after I've moved. "

—*SHANNON*
WIND GAP, PENNSYLVANIA
5 MOVES

. . . .

IT'S WORTH EVERY DIME TO PURCHASE BOXES from a moving company or package/mail store. If the bottom falls out of a used grocery store box as you're crossing the street on a rainy moving day, you will not forgive yourself for penny pinching, and if it happens to someone helping you move, it is exponentially worse.

—*MARY*
IOWA CITY, IOWA
5 MOVES

DON'T EVER ATTEMPT TO PACK CLOTHES away or else you'll get stuck with rain or other weather conditions you wished that you had an outfit or shoes for.

—*SHEILA RAZZAQ*
PALATINE, ILLINOIS
9 *MOVES*

* * * * * * * *

WHEN YOU PACK YOUR STUFF, keep in mind how you'll need to unpack. If you'll need an item, such as your telephone, right after you move in, pack it last at the back of the truck. But just in case everything goes wrong with your move, pack an "emergency bag" and keep it with you, not in the truck. Fill it with a change of clothes, pajamas, toiletries, medicines, and difficult-to-replace items such as your social security card, birth certificate, credit cards, and special jewelry.

—*ELOISE MILLIKEN*
CALIFON, NEW JERSEY
12 *MOVES*

* * * * * * * *

PACK THE HEAVY STUFF ON THE BOTTOM and label the box "this side up." It doesn't work if you're using movers, but friends are usually pretty good at following directions.

—*J.A.*
DURHAM, NORTH CAROLINA
16 *MOVES*

YOU DON'T NEED TO BUY LOTS OF BOXES. Save money by just going to your local supermarket or drug store. Talk to the manager and find out about when they unload shipments and have boxes, and they'll give them to you for free. As long as you don't take boxes that held produce, they'll be clean, sturdy and great for moving.

—*MATT W.*
SAN CARLOS, CALIFORNIA
3 MOVES

. . . .

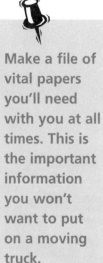

Make a file of vital papers you'll need with you at all times. This is the important information you won't want to put on a moving truck.

—*THE UNOFFICIAL GUIDE TO BUYING A HOME*

WHEN YOU'RE PACKING it would be great to list every single thing that's inside each box on the outside of the box. But that's often just not practical, or even possible. Instead, I label each box with a letter: A, B, C, etc. Then I list each box's letter and its contents on a sheet of paper. For example, box A might contain my coffeemaker, cooking utensils, cutting board, knife block, etc. This makes it easy to find things without ripping open every box!

—*ELLEN*
PITTSBURGH, PENNSYLVANIA
11 MOVES

. . . .

66 Don't get stuck looking through old love letters. This will make your move take much longer and make you sadder to leave. Just pack it up!

—*SARAH KRUMHOLZ*
SAN FRANCISCO, CALIFORNIA
5 MOVES

GETTING PACKED UP WAS THE HARDEST PART because there just isn't time in the day. We were going to use vacation time to do it but then decided not to waste it on that. I think you have to make yourself do it in the evenings after work. If you have trouble finding the energy, make some really, really strong coffee. And tell yourself this is the last time you're moving.

> —*TANYA WEST*
> *FROSTBURG, MARYLAND*
> *5 MOVES*

• • • • • • • •

DON'T MAKE THE MISTAKE OF UNNECESSARILY pulling all of your clothes off of their hangers and packing them, only to hang them back up in your new home. Secure a bundle of clothes on hangers together with a rubber band, and then cover the bundle with a garbage bag to protect them. When you move in, you can just hang them up and tear off the bag.

> —*J.H.*
> *CHICAGO, ILLINOIS*
> *4 MOVES*

ROOM FOR A BROOM?

My mother-in-law and her family have this superstition where you are not allowed to take your broom with you to your new place. Have you ever heard of something so ridiculous? It's supposed to be bad luck. The broom was one of the last things left in my old place because we were using it to clean. When I tried to take it she told me about the superstition. I played along, but after she left I threw it in the truck. That's all I need on top of everything else is to have to buy a new broom.

> —*PATTY KRAMER*
> *PITTSBURGH, PENNSYLVANIA*
> *5 MOVES*

INVEST IN BUBBLE WRAP! Sure, you could wrap all of your breakables in old newspapers, but that leaves behind messy newspaper ink. Plus it really doesn't protect things much. Instead I bought a roll of bubble wrap at Wal-Mart. I wrapped all of my dishes and delicate items in it. Not a single thing was broken on my move!

—BRANDI SMITH
DuBois, PENNSYLVANIA
1 MOVE

• • • • • • • •

"Schedule a 'packing party' with friends and neighbors the weekend before you move, and turn a monotonous task into a party. Have drinks and pizza for everyone and let people help."

—SHONDA J. WAXMAN
SAN JOSE, CALIFORNIA
4 MOVES

• • • • • • • •

I RECOMMEND LABELING YOUR electronic cords when disconnecting things for a move. I would put a piece of tape at the end of each cord and label it with a number or letter and then put a piece of tape near the outlet where the plug belongs and label it with the same symbol. That way, things won't be confusing when it's time to reconnect.

—D.L.
CHICAGO, ILLINOIS
8 MOVES

IF YOU'RE MOVING ABROAD, don't bother bringing electrical appliances. When we moved, I brought the VCR and DVD player and even a mixer and waffle maker. Then I purchased a converter. It was a disaster! The converter was difficult to use, and my waffle maker was fried along with it. The mixer never worked at all. And the converter wasn't powerful enough for the VCR and DVD player. In the end, I just bought everything abroad. It was a little more expensive, but at least I can have waffles again!

—*BETH*
OKLAHOMA
8 MOVES

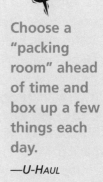

Choose a "packing room" ahead of time and box up a few things each day.

—*U-HAUL*

- - - - - - - -

ATTENTION BOOK COLLECTORS: Don't fill up your boxes with books. Even a medium-sized box filled with books will be terribly heavy. Instead, line the bottom of your boxes with books, and then put lighter items on top of the books to fill the box up.

—*STEVE DAMON*

- - - - - - - -

NEVER UNDERESTIMATE HOW MUCH STUFF you have. You will think that most of your packing is done when the furniture is gone. But you still have at least one more truckload to pack. Sure, it may seem like all you have left is a broom and dust-pan in your closet, some clothes in the bedroom, some small boxes in the basement, and a few items in the garage, but watch out. Your junk will multiply in number and weight as you move from room to room.

—*JOHN SEYER*
LOVELAND, COLORADO
3 MOVES

PUTTING THINGS IN ORDER

ALWAYS START BY PACKING THE KITCHEN and all the knick-knacks everywhere in the house—the china, crystal, and stuff in the kitchen you don't need to use every day. The decorative items on coffee tables, shelves, etc., can be done early, too. The good thing about doing it this way is you will be more likely to wrap them well and nicely because you're not too tired and are focused on protecting the breakables. Books would be next—they are easy, quick and you don't need them regularly. Then comes clothing in drawers or on shelves that you don't wear all the time or in that season. By the time you get through with that, you're mostly done.

> —*ALLISON T. LEVYN*
> *BEVERLY HILLS, CALIFORNIA*
> 🚚 *4 MOVES*

TAKE THE SMALL STUFF FIRST, and group it in boxes according to where the stuff was from. For example, I had a box of everything from my nightstand.

> —*JENNIFER BRIGHT REICH*
> *HELLERTOWN, PENNSYLVANIA*
> 🚚 *6 MOVES*

START PACKING ALL THE THINGS you won't have any immediate need for on a daily basis as soon as you know you'll be moving—things like books, CDs, knick-knacks, off-season clothing and sports equipment. Wait to pack the most essential things—cookware, clothes you wear often, bathroom supplies, etc.—until a few days before you move.

> —*D.T.*
> *LOS ANGELES, CALIFORNIA*
> 🚚 *4 MOVES*

DO NOT PACK UNTIL YOU ONLY HAVE A FEW days left before the move. You still have to exist daily, y'know? Have an extra box or three on hand when you do start . . . You have not packed everything. No, you haven't. I promise.

—CHRISTINA SCHELIN
BELMONT, MASSACHUSETTS
7 MOVES

. . . .

Tape BOTH sides of the box. Sure, it's funny when someone picks up a box and all the stuff falls out of the bottom, but not when it's your stuff.

—DANNY GALLAGHER
HENDERSON, TEXAS
3 MOVES

. . . .

SET ASIDE A BOX FOR YOUR REMOTE CONTROLS, a tool kit and a phone—anything you need right away. This should be the last box you pack and the first box you open at your new place. It's great because you don't waste time digging through a dozen boxes to find the important stuff.

—ROB MCHARGUE
SAN ANTONIO, TEXAS
10 MOVES

ALWAYS KEEP BEAUTY AND FACE PRODUCTS with you. If you can't wash your face, that's the worst thing. Plus, when you move somewhere new, you want to look your best.

—SHEILA RAZZAQ
PALATINE, ILLINOIS
9 MOVES

• • • • • • • •

FOR EACH ROOM, put only the essentials you'll need for the first three days in one box, and label it "Kitchen, immediately." Everything else that belongs in the kitchen but isn't crucial, put in other boxes marked "Kitchen, storage." When you arrive at your new place, put only the essential boxes in each room. Once you get them cleaned out, then move everything else in. The house won't feel like a disaster area this way.

—BARB ZAHN
FRANKTOWN, COLORADO
10 MOVES

• • • • • • • •

START AS EARLY AS YOU CAN PACKING UP nonessentials, things you don't need to use for daily living, including winter clothes if it's summer (and vice versa), the broiler plate you use only once in a blue moon and so on. I usually try to start at least 4 weekends in advance, so I can do a few hours each weekend instead of going nuts 2 days before the move date.

—ANNETTE C. YOUNG
VANCOUVER, WASHINGTON
8 MOVES

• • • • • • • •

IF AT ALL POSSIBLE, keep the original boxes for fragile items when you purchase them; it is easier to reuse these boxes than risk breaking the items during a move.

—LARA LOEST
MILWAUKEE, WISCONSIN
6 MOVES

THE BEST THING ABOUT MOVING is it's like thrift shopping in your own home. Whenever I move out I always discover some skirt or tank top that's been hidden behind my dresser for years. Had I known it was there, I would have donated it. But now, it's been so long that it's actually back in style, retro-cool, and I've got a new outfit to go with my new apartment!

—CARIN DAVIS
LOS ANGELES, CALIFORNIA

Pack your pillows in boxes. I used to make the mistake of just throwing pillows in the back of the truck for padding, but they got so dirty and gross I had to throw them away.

—ASHLEY KNOTTS
ANDERSON, INDIANA
10 MOVES

I'VE GOTTEN REALLY GOOD AT MAKING LISTS, on which I write down everything from my bank account numbers, to my passwords, to little reminders about what debts I still need to pay off. Moving is so hectic, and it's easy to forget something "minor," like a bill for a magazine subscription. But these things can end up on your credit report and come back to haunt you.

—ANNA LONDON
MELBOURNE, AUSTRALIA
3 MOVES

PACKING TAPE CAN BE EXTREMELY DIFFICULT to remove from picture frames, glass, and bubble wrap. Use tape as sparingly as possible, while maintaining the security of your objects.

—*ANONYMOUS*
BIRMINGHAM, ALABAMA
6 MOVES

" **Put cleaning items in a separate box or bag and make sure the lids are on tight. I once forgot to do this, and dishwashing soap ended up spilling over a dozen books.** "

—*SARAH CLARK*
NEW YORK, NEW YORK
9 MOVES

WHEN I MOVED TO DENVER FOR LAW SCHOOL, I had to downsize. I borrowed my dad's Volvo station wagon and decided that whatever fit in there, I could keep. I selected the one piece of furniture I couldn't live without, as well as basic luxury items, like my stereo and TV. I also included practical things, like dishes. It helped tremendously to have this simple goal because it forced me to consider what I truly needed, as opposed to what I was emotionally attached to.

—*LIBBY DEBLASIO*
DENVER, COLORADO
7 MOVES

MAKE THAT A DOUBLE KNOT

EVERYONE HAS THEIR "UNMENTIONABLE" ITEMS—particularly couples. You know what I mean? Various paraphernalia for after-dark play? Just make triple-sure you pack up these things in a super-secret box and tape it shut 27 times over. Especially if you're having your neighbor help you move. We forgot to make these arrangements. Instead, we left our "unmentionable" items in a drawer of our nightstand. The drawer was taped shut. But wouldn't you know it—my helpful neighbor came strolling out of the house with that night-  stand, and just as he arrived at the moving van and said, "Where do you want this?" the tape ripped and the drawer tumbled open. There, on the driveway, rested you know what. And to add a level of surreal perver- sion to it, a Holy Bible was among the items. We've never even opened a single page of that bible—particularly while using those other items. But seeing it all together, there was nothing to do but wait for the awkward silence to pass before picking every- thing up.

> —JWAIII
> ATLANTA, GEORGIA
> 15 MOVES

. . . .

TAKE YOUR TIME PACKING. Get boxes. Don't just throw everything everywhere. Get labels. Get big black markers and bubble wrap. Don't wrap stuff in towels. It always breaks.

> —LAURA BATOG
> FRANKLIN, MASSACHUSETTS
> 4 MOVES

To make dreaded tasks more enjoyable, listen to music while performing the task, or give yourself a reward after.

—*The One-Minute Organizer*

TAKE ALL OF YOUR T-SHIRTS AND USE THEM to pad your dishes and other breakable things. Then get a box of garbage bags. Leaf bags, to be precise. The heavy ones. Pack everything else that is soft in them (clothes, linens, pillows, whatever) and use them to pad your moving vehicle.

—*Sarah*
Seattle, Washington
15 moves

• • • • • • • •

BEFORE YOU START PACKING, get a layout of your new house and number every single room—master bedroom is 1, kitchen is 2, dining room is 3, etc. Then, while loading up the boxes, subcategorize using ABCs for specific items: "A" might be clothing, "B" might be toys, "C" might be cleaning supplies, etc. If you want to be even more specific, add a third category—your first initial. Using this system, boxes labeled 1AR would be my clothing for the master bedroom, since my name is Rick.

—*Rick Rush*
Littleton, Colorado
7 moves

• • • • • • • •

IF YOU'RE MOVING A LONG DISTANCE and hire a moving company, be sure to take your vacuum and other cleaning supplies with you in the car. We arrived several days before our stuff, so I was able to vacuum the floor, where we were sleeping, and thoroughly clean our home before all of our belongings arrived. How often in life do you get the chance to clean a completely empty house?! Seize that opportunity any time you can!

—*Tori Dennis*
Iron City, Tennessee
5 moves

BE SURE THAT EVERYTHING IS MARKED, especially the stuff you need right away. Make sure you can find your kitchen and bathroom stuff and your sheets. I printed out labels on my computer that said exactly what was in the boxes, even if the movers had packed it.

—*CHRISTINE BEIDEL*
RUTHERFORD, NEW JERSEY
2 MOVES

• • • • • • • •

❝Resist the temptation to drop something in a box without listing it on the outside. Next thing you know, you've lost your checkbook.❞

—*RANDALL HARRIS*
BROOKLYN, NEW YORK
10 MOVES

• • • • • • • •

I'M ONE OF THOSE WEIRDOS who *loves* to move. When I pack stuff, I'm very meticulous. Each box has a particular place to go. Each one is marked—kitchen, garage, bathroom, master bedroom, and so on. I pack the moving truck in reverse order of how I'm going to walk through the new house unpacking. It's easier and faster to unpack that way. I do the upstairs first, so I get the physically harder portion out of the way while I still have plenty of energy. I label everything, so if someone has a question about where something goes, I ask, "What does the box say?"

—*KEVIN SCHWARZ*
FORT COLLINS, COLORADO
4 MOVES

> ## " Always wait until the last minute. It'll eventually get done, so why drag it out? "

—*M.H.*
MINNEAPOLIS, MINNESOTA
2 MOVES

• • • • • • • •

A WEEK'S WORTH OF CLOTHING and any medications or pills should always ride with you, regardless of whether you're driving or flying. Not just for the obvious reason (so they don't get lost). What happens if you're bumped off a flight and forced to spend 24 hours somewhere?

—*KATHY MCCLINTIC*
CENTENNIAL, COLORADO
2 MOVES

Out With the Old: To Trash or To Cash?

Hold on a second: You're not really going to pack THAT thing, are you? Or should we say, RE-pack it, since it's been packed away since your last move? One of the keys to a successful move is to leave things behind. Trash them. Or sell them. Or give them away. Less can be more. Having trouble letting go? Read on for tips on how to hock the items that clog your life, or just get rid of a few things you don't really need.

YOU WILL FIND NEW STUFF, and I am a big believer in making things easier for yourself. It is just *stuff* anyway.

> —*LEO*
> *LOS ANGELES, CALIFORNIA*
> 5 MOVES

IF YOU HAVEN'T TOUCHED SOMETHING IN 10 YEARS, THROW IT OUT!

> —*ANDREW*
> *EVANSTON, ILLINOIS*
> 5 MOVES

Throwing things away is a great alternative to packing.

—*ANONYMOUS*
ALEXANDRIA,
VIRGINIA
3 MOVES

LOOK AT THE MOVE AS IF YOUR HOUSE BURNED down in a fire. Ask yourself: If you came back in after a fire what would you most hope was not burned? Take those things. Moving is a good chance to get rid of things you really didn't want in the first place.

—*DAN BLANDO*
FROSTBURG, MARYLAND
2 MOVES

• • • • • • • •

WHEN YOU'RE PACKING and you find a box that's still packed from the last time you moved, throw it out. You obviously don't need anything in it. I found a box like that the last time I moved, and I opened it up to see what was inside. It was, of course, total crap, and I wondered, "Why did I bother moving this junk the last time?!"

—*J.B.*
SAN FRANCISCO, CALIFORNIA
12 MOVES

• • • • • • • •

NEVER MOVE UNIVERSITY BOOKS. If you really want to reference something from your social history class, you can always buy new textbooks on Amazon for peanuts (and you'll get the better, updated version!).

—*MICHAEL GARRITY*
TORONTO, ONTARIO, CANADA
10 MOVES

• • • • • • • •

CLUTTER'S LAST STAND is one of my favorite books . . . I try to throw out/donate all kinds of stuff before I move. This allows me to move fewer boxes, is less expensive, and less time consuming in the end.

—*ELIZABETH BONET*
SUNRISE, FLORIDA
13 MOVES

IT IS NOT WORTH THE TIME AND EFFORT to have a garage sale. I think we made a profit of $250 for a whole day's work and still had tons of stuff left over that we had to deal with anyway. Just donate it all to Goodwill or the Salvation Army and take the tax deduction. Faster, easier, more philanthropic, and just as profitable in the end.

     —M.S.
       NEW YORK, NEW YORK
       4 MOVES

• • • • • • • •

" Old clothes can be taken to the Salvation Army. Old CDs can be sold back to the record store. Old pictures of your ex can be burned ceremonially in the living room. "

     —R.G.
       CHICAGO, ILLINOIS

• • • • • • • •

WHEN I MOVED FROM IOWA TO IDAHO for a job, I had only about $100 to my name, so I had to be as low-budget as possible, which meant getting rid of everything I owned that I couldn't fit in the back of my tiny Mustang. Only true necessities made the cut: books, clothes, CDs, computer, TV and that's about it. Everything else went either into the trash or to Goodwill. I had that Mustang as packed as any Mustang has been packed before.

     —JEREMY SCHNITKER
       COUNCIL BLUFFS, IOWA
       5 MOVES

MEN ARE FROM MARS . . .

Men should be allowed to keep some things, and my wife has been gracious in allowing this. I keep dozens of old Playboy magazines that belonged to my dad, for instance. They're from the '60s and are frayed around the edges and heavy to carry in a box. I guess I'm hoping that one day I'll sell them for a fortune on eBay or I'll have some sort of meaningful "Playboy Hand-Me-Down Ceremony" with my son. But until then, I keep them in storage and somehow sleep better this way. I also keep old video game systems. I have an Atari 2600 that still plays games from the late '70s and early '80s. I also have the original Nintendo  Entertainment System. Once in a blue moon, I hook one up to the television and I relive the glory of lost youth. I think my wife realizes that these are things that should not be relegated to the trash can.

—JWAIII
ATLANTA, GEORGIA
15 MOVES

AFTER I MOVED FROM SAN DIEGO TO CHICAGO,
I made it a rule to clean out my house every year
as if I was moving across the country. Now I
regularly throw things out. People keep too many
things they don't need. You feel so much more in
control of your life when things are organized
and cleaned out.

> —J.R.
> CHICAGO, ILLINOIS
> 5 MOVES

• • • • • • • •

CONSIDER THE VALUE OF YOUR FURNITURE, especially
if it's a long move or a multi-state move. You can
knock off a lot of the cost, time, effort and
aggravation if you get rid of some of your bigger
pieces. I calculated how much it would cost to
move and store my furniture. Even if I had rented
a U-Haul, it was cheaper just to sell it to my
roommate and buy new stuff later.

> —SARAH SPARKS
> WASHINGTON, DC
> 8 MOVES

• • • • • • • •

IF YOU'RE MOVING ABROAD TEMPORARILY, prioritize
the stuff you put in storage "1" through "5," with
"1" being the things you absolutely want to keep
and "5" being if it hits the dumpster, you're not
going to think twice. That way, if you decide to
stay longer, your friends can go into your storage
unit and easily throw stuff out or mail it to you.

> —J.C.
> REDMOND, WASHINGTON
> 15 MOVES

• • • • • • • •

NEXT TIME, I'LL RENT A DUMPSTER. Everything
goes either in the moving van or in the dumpster.

> —JEANNE ECKMAN
> LANCASTER, PENNSYLVANIA
> 2 MOVES

Consider using
a tag sale to
get rid of your
stuff. A tag
sale operator
will manage
the entire
event and give
you about 25
percent of the
sale's income.

> —THE EVERYTHING
> HOMESELLING
> BOOK

MOVE EVERYTHING! When I left a long-term relationship, I moved most of my things but not all of them. This has become a huge problem. My former boyfriend and I aren't on good terms, and it has been very hard to make arrangements for me to get my things back. My advice: If you're going, take it all with you!

—*L.G.K.*
EASTON, PENNSYLVANIA
5 MOVES

. . . .

"Don't give away all your possessions. You will regret it. When I went to the army, I gave my favorite peace pipe to a girl. I thought I would never smoke again, but actually, I would like to."

—*DANIEL LARSON*
DES PLAINS, ILLINOIS
5 MOVES

. . . .

SCHEDULE A GARAGE SALE A MONTH BEFORE your move so you can get rid of the old rugs, clothing, and household items that don't need to move with you. After the sale, take everything left over to Goodwill or a local charity—immediately. You'll get a good tax write-off and will have much less to pack.

—*SHONDA J. WAXMAN*
SAN JOSE, CALIFORNIA
4 MOVES

WHILE A LOT OF PEOPLE HAVE A YARD SALE, I think it's easiest to call your local Salvation Army, Goodwill or a similar charitable organization. Many of them will come pick up and transport your discarded items for you, so it is more convenient than taking the goods to a second-hand store and less time consuming than a yard sale. Plus, you have the opportunity to give your stuff to people who really need it.

> —*T. HUTCHINS*
> *BARLING, ARKANSAS*
> 6 *MOVES*

• • • • • • • •

I DON'T THINK I'M A PACKRAT. But the rats have a different opinion.

> —*S.G.*
> *SYRACUSE, NEW YORK*
> 2 *MOVES*

• • • • • • • •

I LIKE HAVING A SPRING CLEAN before I move because I like to make a fresh start in my new place. When I moved to Australia, I donated/sold clothes and books and other replaceable items, gave my furniture to friends to use while I was away. I also threw out lots of junk I'd been uselessly hanging onto (notes from college and several years' worth of birthday cards). This was a fairly ruthless thing to do, but my minimalist attitude is still going strong 4 years later.

> —*NICOLE HOWARD*
> *SEATTLE, WASHINGTON*
> 6 *MOVES*

• • • • • • • •

DON'T BRING OLD PHOTOS OF YOUR BOYFRIENDS. If you're broken up, chances are you won't need them again!

> —*JEAN ROBERTSON*
> *GLENVIEW, ILLINOIS*
> 3 *MOVES*

To begin clearing clutter, start with the easiest stuff—things that don't require decision-making on your part. Grab a trash bag and start throwing it away.

> —*THE ONE-MINUTE ORGANIZER*

DON'T TAKE CLOTHES with you that you haven't worn within the last four months.

—*N.L.*
CHICAGO, ILLINOIS
3 MOVES

· · · · · · · ·

I DON'T LET ANYONE TELL ME that I should throw stuff out. It's my stuff and I'll keep it if I want to. Everyone wants to tell you that you have too much stuff. I'll make that decision.

—*WILLIAM GREEN*
FROSTBURG, MARYLAND
1 MOVE

· · · · · · · ·

THROW AWAY EVERYTHING. I once had a job cleaning out someone's house after they died and it took days to haul out all of the junk they had probably never looked at.

—*DAN LESSIN*
HELOTES, TEXAS
20 MOVES

· · · · · · · ·

What is so important that you can't move on without it?

—*JOHN STANLEY*
EAST PALESTINE, OHIO

I'M AGAINST YARD SALES IN ANY SITUATION, but especially during a move. You are not thinking clearly at that point because of the stress of moving, and you'd be willing to sell stuff then that you wouldn't ordinarily. Plus, do you really want all your neighbors coming over and browsing through your personal belongings?

—*E.J.P.*
CRANBERRY TOWNSHIP, PENNSYLVANIA
2 MOVES

· · · · · · · ·

PRICE THINGS LOW IF YOU HAVE A YARD SALE. Don't try to make money off this. Just get rid of stuff.

—*J.V.*
RANDOLPH, VERMONT
7 MOVES

PUTTING A PRICE ON JUNK

WHEN I MOVED FROM NEW MEXICO TO ARIZONA, I had so much crap that it took me two trips. Because my new place was smaller than my old one, I rented a storage area in my new hometown to keep my extra stuff in. For four years, I paid $35 a month to house everything. One day, I realized how much money I was wasting—$1,680 in all!—and this motivated me to throw out everything I hadn't used in the past six months.

Today, the only items in storage are my tools, camping equipment, Christmas stuff and a few collectibles.

> —MARK SCOTT
> SAFFORD, ARIZONA
> 10 MOVES

• • • • • • • • •

YOU SHOULD WEIGH STUFF AND LEARN THE COST of shipping it. I have a big rock that I keep moving, which actually cost me $20 to ship. If you put a price on it, it'll help you decide if it's worth it.

> —ANONYMOUS
> TORONTO, ONTARIO, CANADA
> 10 MOVES

I ONCE MADE THE MISTAKE OF BRINGING a collage an ex-girlfriend made me and it drove me crazy—I was 400 miles away and knew I could never see her again. But somehow, it still tortured me seeing something she made for me.

—*ANDREW*
EVANSTON, ILLINOIS
5 MOVES

I gave away a really nice stereo. I still regret that.

—*DOMINIQUE*
COLEMAN
SYRACUSE,
NEW YORK
5 MOVES

BE CAREFUL OF THOSE WOMEN who will negotiate with you so much that all of the sudden you are paying them to take your garage-sale items.

—*E.T.*
PORTLAND, MAINE
4 MOVES

I THINK IT'S REALLY HEALTHY TO MOVE 2 or 3 times so you can survey and document everything you've accumulated and get rid of a lot of it. Last time my wife and I moved, we were required to spend almost a year with about 10 percent of our possessions. It made us realize that moving is nature's way of getting you to return to a simple and good life.

—*TOM W.*
LENOX, MASSACHUSETTS

I RECOMMEND DONATING AS MUCH AS YOU CAN. Give old sheets and towels to the SPCA. Donate magazines and books to hospitals and nursing homes. Offer kitchen supplies to women's crisis centers, which often help women set up their own apartments. And take clothes, appliances, and toys to the Salvation Army or thrift charities.

—*JEAN NICK*
KINTNERSVILLE, PENNSYLVANIA
10 MOVES

BEFORE MY LAST MOVE, I spent a month weeding through my possessions and files after files of paper, filling Hefty bag after Hefty bag. One of the most positive aspects of moving is that it allows you to get rid of all of the stuff you've been collecting, discard that old pair of jeans from college that will NEVER fit again, and start anew. Sure, the stuff accumulates all over again but methodical purging is a healing ritual in its own right.

—*LIZ SCHERER*
ANNAPOLIS, MARYLAND
 *3 MOVES*

• • • • • • • •

> You don't need to bring clothes from the last decade of your life. Chances are they're too small and definitely out of style.

—*NATALIE*
EVANSTON, ILLINOIS
5 MOVES

• • • • • • • •

YOU MAY HAVE T-SHIRTS THAT REMIND YOU of certain things that happened in the past, but do you ever wear them? And if you have things that are honest-to-goodness mementos and you don't want to part with them, is having them stacked in drawers or piled in closets the best way to keep them? If it isn't being used or actually adding to the decor, then get rid of it.

—*A.H.*
STURGIS, MICHIGAN
9 MOVES

OLD STUFF, NEW MONEY

Letting go of those golf clubs you used twice, the angora sweater Aunt Gert gave you for your 16th birthday, and the waffle maker you never took out of the box can be traumatic. But getting some good, hard cash in return will ease the pain. Here's advice from some happy hockers.

ALWAYS KNOW WHERE A GOOD CONSIGNMENT SHOP IS. I've made so much money selling my things instead of just throwing away old items that I thought were useless. There is always someone else willing to buy your used stuff—and you can profit from it!

    —*SARA FAIWELL*
      BUFFALO GROVE, ILLINOIS
      7 MOVES

• • • • • • • •

YOU'RE NOT GOING TO WANT TO HAVE A GARAGE sale after you're all packed up and ready to move. It's just the last thing on your mind. If possible, join in someone else's garage sale. A larger sale will bring in more customers.

    —*ELLIS*
      SEATTLE, WASHINGTON
      9 MOVES

• • • • • • • •

IF YOU'RE GOING TO DO IT, DO IT RIGHT. Advertise beforehand and make sure you have good stuff for sale (furniture, collectibles, etc.) so that you bring in the real garage sale aficionados. Then, I suggest having a half-off sale for the last hour or so. And take just about any price for the last 15 minutes. At that point, it's better just to get rid of things and get some money than have to pack it all up.

    —*J.W.*
      ROCHESTER, NEW YORK
      14 MOVES

YARD SALES SERVE TWO GOOD PURPOSES when you're moving. First, the more you sell, the less you have to move. Second, every little bit of extra cash helps when you are moving. I took the money I made from my last pre-move yard sale and used it for all the little stuff I had to buy—like cleaning supplies and food for my friends who moved me.

    —*DEBBIE PRZYWARTY*
    IRWIN, PENNSYLVANIA
    3 MOVES

HAVE AN AUCTION/PRIVATE TAG SALE. Invite your friends or coworkers over for a potluck dinner and sell things you don't want to move. Tell them it's going toward the moving fund. Have fun and look at it as a way to clean without sitting alone in a room with garbage bags. Be prepared to be embarrassed about the junk you are dumping on them, be fair with prices, and enjoy getting rid of things someone else can use.

    —*JILL*
    WEEHAWKEN, NEW JERSEY
    12 MOVES

I HAVE A 2-YEAR RULE—if I haven't worn it, used it, looked at it, opened it or read it in 2 years, it is given or thrown away. Since most of my moves are less than 2 years apart, it is relatively easy and keeps the excess to a minimum.

—*TINA MUSIAL*
MATAWAN, NEW JERSEY
6 MOVES

. . . .

" Be brutal with your culling. There's nothing worse than unpacking something at the new place and realizing that you don't need it and that you paid someone to move stuff that should have been in the garage sale or give-away pile. "

—*HAROLD JAFFE*
REDMOND, WASHINGTON
9 MOVES

. . . .

IF YOU ALREADY HAVE SOME STORAGE SPACE, move as much there as you can before the big moving day. That way, you aren't under any time pressure to get the things in or out of there. On moving day, it's not as traumatic because you aren't bringing and unpacking everything you own.

—*CLYDE FORRESTER*
FOREST PARK, ILLINOIS
7 MOVES

DONATE THINGS YOU HAVE NOT USED, opened, listened to, read, worn or touched for six months. You can always find another one. Last year I donated Christmas gift wrap and half-used boxes of cards to a retirement home and they were thrilled. Give craft supplies to a Girl Scout troop or elementary school. Donate books to a library or neighborhood center. Donate gently worn clothes to Dress for Success or a shelter. Never read those *Gourmet* or *Bon Appetit* magazines? Tear out the five pages you want to keep from each one, put them in a folder and recycle the rest. Then cancel your subscription.

> —ANONYMOUS
> WEEHAWKEN, NEW JERSEY
> 12 MOVES

Have at least two people "working" the sale, one of whom is capable of negotiating price.

> —HOMEDEPOT
> MOVING.COM

• • • • • • • •

MY WIFE AND I HAVE ALWAYS PARKED the moving truck next to the dumpster. As you walk down the stairs, you're forced to make a key decision about just how much you REALLY want that item.

> —DARIN WATKINS
> PALOUSE, WASHINGTON
> 20 MOVES

• • • • • • • •

I USED TO BE A HUGE PACKRAT, until I had to move all my earthly belongings from Iowa to California in a Honda Accord. The unforgiving nature of the Honda's trunk and back-seat forced me to part with many items that I once considered vital. Since then, I have somehow managed to carry on my existence without old *Sports Illustrated* magazines and note-books from high school Spanish classes.

> —J.A.
> LOS ANGELES, CALIFORNIA
> 7 MOVES

DON'T PACK FOOD. Give it away. My aunt moved across the country with 10 boxes of canned goods. It was out of control.

—*K. BECKERING*
SYRACUSE, NEW YORK
4 MOVES

• • • • • • • •

I'LL GIVE STUFF AWAY to friends/relatives if they want it and I'm not taking it with me.

—*BEV WALTON-PORTER*
COLORADO SPRINGS, COLORADO
7 MOVES

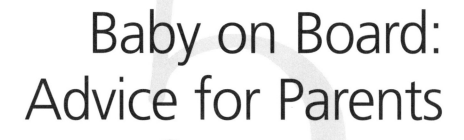

Baby on Board: Advice for Parents

As a parent, you realize that just about everything revolves around your kids. So when you are planning something as life-altering as a move, you have to be prepared for how the children will take it. They may be scared about starting a new school or worried about leaving their playmates behind, and they may absolutely flip out when Teddy or Barbie gets boxed up. Here are some tips on making the move more bearable for the little ones.

ONCE THE MOVE WAS COMPLETE I made sure the kids had their rooms set up with their things in it. Making sure they had familiar things around them even made *me* feel better.

—*C.P.*
MONMOUTH BEACH, NEW JERSEY
 *4 MOVES*

HIRE A BABYSITTER FOR THE MOVING DAYS.

—*SUSAN M.*
CHICAGO, ILLINOIS
4 MOVES

SEE JANE MOVE

MY DAUGHTER WAS 7 WHEN WE MOVED from California to Sweden. A psychologist recommended making a "moving book" for her. I bought a blank book that also had pockets and I wrote a story that explained the move in a step-by-step way. I printed out clip art to paste on the appropriate pages, etc.

She and I started reading this book a couple of weeks before the actual move. I bought lots of film for our old Polaroid camera and she got to take pictures that day and put them in the pockets of the book. There was space on each page for her to write about her feelings. It was still pretty traumatic for all of us, but I'm convinced that preparing for the move by describing it in a very explicit and concrete way helped her to understand what was happening.

> —DEBORAH BRANSCUM
> STOCKHOLM, SWEDEN
> 4 MOVES

. . . .

WE MOVED WHEN OUR KIDS WERE 8 AND 2. I bought books for both of them about moving. The oldest got a book you could fill in with things about the old house and friends to remember them and the youngest got picture books about moving. Reading them really helped. We also gave the oldest a camera and let her take photos of anything she wanted at the old house.

> —BRETTE SEMBER
> CLARENCE, NEW YORK
> 4 MOVES

BEFORE WE MOVED, we discussed it with our children, who were 11 and 9 at the time. We realized that it would change all of our lives, so we made them a part of the decision in everything from selecting a house and school abroad to packing. It made them feel really grown up. And it made the whole move much easier knowing that we were doing this as a family.

> —*JAYNE J.*
> *TULSA, OKLAHOMA*
> 🚚 *1 TIME*

· · · · · · · ·

A FUN THING THAT THE KIDS and I did to help us make our new house feel like home was to camp out in the living room. We had no furniture in the living room for a while after we moved in, and one long weekend in January we had no heat. So we got out our sleeping bags, kept a fire going in the fireplace, set up the radio, and pretended we were camping.

> —*K.M. CARTER*
> *DES MOINES, IOWA*
> 🚚 *7 MOVES*

· · · · · · · ·

WHEN WE WERE BUILDING A NEW HOUSE, I asked the builder's rep if she knew of any other families building in our development who had kids our age. She found some, got their permission, and we exchanged phone numbers so the kids could meet before school started. It helped a lot. Also, although our house wasn't done when school started, I drove my son to the bus stop in our new neighborhood every day, so he could get to know the other kids on the street and on the bus. By the time we moved in a month later, he was totally settled in.

> —*AMY REA*
> *EDEN PRAIRIE, MINNESOTA*
> 🚚 *6 MOVES*

Our two-year-old loved bubble-wrap, so we just let her go and play.

> —*J.B.*
> *EAST SYRACUSE,*
> *NEW YORK*
> 🚚 *6 MOVES*

WE MOVED TO A NEW HOUSE IN THE SAME CITY, when our oldest was about to turn 4. I drove him past the new house so many times before we actually moved in, the neighbors probably thought we were stalkers. But by the time moving day arrived, he was really excited and didn't feel apprehensive at all because it was already so familiar. He had already come to think of it as "his" house.
—PAULA ANDRUSS

• • • • • • • •

WE MADE OUR KIDS RIDE THE BUS HOME from school. I knew it would help them get to know kids in the neighborhood. I was right. My daughter met a girl who would soon become her best friend. They're going to room together at college next year.
—PAT CURRY
WATKINSVILLE, GEORGIA
4 MOVES

• • • • • • • •

IF YOUR KIDS ARE OLDER, discuss the pros and cons of moving with them. We sat down with our kids a couple of times at meals and made a list of what they were anxious about, versus what they were looking forward to. Then, after being here a few months we referred back to the lists. We asked them, "Has this turned out to be true, this thing you were worried about?" It gave them a way of keeping track of themselves. It was helpful to me, too.
—E.T.
PORTLAND, MAINE
4 MOVES

YOU CAN'T AFFORD NOT TO HIRE A BABYSITTER
for a move. When we moved out, I was so
preoccupied with my son that I wasn't able to
pay attention to the movers as carefully as I
should have, and they ended up breaking a very
expensive vase. On the move in, he was totally
underfoot, and he just missed having a heavy box
topple on him. I could imagine a kid getting
seriously hurt on moving day.

> —SUSAN M.
> CHICAGO, ILLINOIS
> 4 MOVES

• • • • • • • •

**" Let the kids pick two or three
stuffed animals and a blanket
to travel with them, outside the
moving van. "**

> —SUSIE WALTON
> SAN DIEGO, CALIFORNIA
> 7 MOVES

• • • • • • • •

ASK A RELATIVE WHO'S NOT DIRECTLY INVOLVED
with helping you move to take the kids somewhere fun for the day of the move. It gets them
out of the way so they are not underfoot, primar-
ily. But it also keeps them from having any bad
feelings about seeing all your stuff packed up. To
watch that can be traumatic for young kids.
When we moved, my mom took my kids to
the movies all day. When they got back we
were in the new place and they were excited
about it.

> —M.K.M.
> OWINGS, MARYLAND
> 3 MOVES

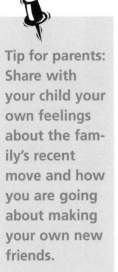

Tip for parents:
Share with
your child your
own feelings
about the fam-
ily's recent
move and how
you are going
about making
your own new
friends.

—EHOW.COM

WE ACTUALLY ASKED OUR DAUGHTER if she wanted to move abroad! We figured that, since she was moving there with us, she should have input into the decision. She was thrilled with the idea of moving abroad and with the fact that we asked for her permission! The roles were reversed and she relished it. She still tells people about how she gave us permission to move to Europe!

—E.G.
NEW HAVEN, CONNECTICUT
3 MOVES

. . . .

MY SON WAS IN FIRST GRADE when we moved and we had a big going-away party in the back yard. I made him business cards on the computer with his name, new address, phone number and picture on the cards. That way, he could pass them out to his friends who he was leaving and give the cards to friends at his new school. It helped him with the whole "leaving his school friends" anxiety.

—*SUZANNE DAUGHERTY*
ARLINGTON HEIGHTS, ILLINOIS
3 MOVES

. . . .

YOU SHOULD PACK A LOT OF THE KIDS' FAVORITE toys in one box. Then when you get to the other end, you let them unpack the box. It's the coolest thing. They think it's like Christmas, because when the movers pack they wrap everything in paper, then the kids have to unwrap it. It works really well—it keeps them occupied for a while.

—*COLLEEN WOZNIAK*
AURORA, ILLINOIS
3 MOVES

A KID'S-EYE VIEW

To be honest, when I first heard about our impending move, I was stressed to the max. How could I leave my friends and familiar surroundings behind? I knew the best shortcut to the Quick Pik, the ditch, and the secret clubhouse. Frustrated, I tried every trick in my how-to-get-your-own-way bag. I held my breath until my eyes bulged out like a frog. I stomped my feet until my legs went numb. I even tried the old, "I'm not eating and you can't make me" trick, all to no avail. We were definitely moving.

Eventually, the sun rose on moving day. I watched in a gloomy fog as the last box was loaded into the van. Life as I knew it was over. The new house, several hundred miles away, was awesome. Not that I cared; I was fully prepared to hate every square inch. Intent upon making everyone feel guilty for ruining my life, I sat hunched and alone by the basement door.

But I was only making myself miserable. Whether I liked it or not, we had moved. Soon, though, I would meet my new best friend. She couldn't tackle like my old friend Steve, but she had the prettiest smile and the biggest bluest eyes I've ever seen.

My advice is to never be afraid of new things; change is sometimes awesome. And, be prepared to meet new friends in the most unexpected places.

—ANDREW MCCORMICK
JACKSONVILLE, FLORIDA
5 MOVES

IF YOU HAVE VERY YOUNG KIDS, it's important for them to know that their new home has things in common with your present home. For example, that the new neighborhood has a McDonald's on the corner, too.

—*SUSIE WALTON*
SAN DIEGO, CALIFORNIA
🚚 *7 MOVES*

• • • • • • • •

GET KIDS INVOLVED IN MOVING by throwing out (or giving away) toys they don't use anymore. Tell them that if they get a huge garbage bag full of toys or games that they will never use, you'll get them something new once you get to the new house.

—*T. OLSEN*
ELMHURST, ILLINOIS
🚚 *3 MOVES*

• • • • • • • •

PARK THE KIDS. When we moved, we sent the kids to my in-laws so they wouldn't be in the way during the move. We left them there so long that my in-laws finally came to our house, not because they wanted to see us, but to get rid of the kids.

—*KEN D.*
ATLANTA, GEORGIA
🚚 *50 MOVES*

• • • • • • • •

MAKE SURE KIDS ARE SAFE ON MOVING DAY. You'll be too busy packing and moving to keep them. It's best to get them out of harm's way so they don't get stressed out, stepped on, or packed up.

—*ELLEN*
PITTSBURGH, PENNSYLVANIA
🚚 *11 MOVES*

WE BROUGHT OUR KIDS TO THE HOUSE every time we came for a walk-through, inspection or whatever, so they felt comfortable here. We also drove by the new school, too. On the day of the move, we kept them at the old house for a couple hours, so that they could really see the truck being loaded and everything going into it. Then my mom came and took them to her house for the day. Once everything was unloaded into the new house, the first thing I did was make their beds and get their rooms somewhat in order. When they came home that night to the new house, their rooms were made up and the things they picked out were waiting for them.

—*BRETTE SEMBER*
CLARENCE, NEW YORK
4 MOVES

• • • • • • • • •

LET THE KIDS PACK A BAG: When we moved from North Carolina to Tennessee a few years ago, my three daughters were only 6, 5, and 3. To make them more comfortable, but not give them too much responsibility, I let them each choose a favorite toy, blanket, and pillow to pack and keep with them in the car. These few objects really helped them in the time before the rest of our things arrived in the moving truck.

—*TORI DENNIS*
IRON CITY, TENNESSEE
5 MOVES

• • • • • • • • •

ENROLL YOUR KIDS IN SPORTS TEAMS soon after you arrive. If your kids aren't sporty, they could join something like the chess club. And if there isn't a club for your kids' interest, start one.

—*SUSIE WALTON*
SAN DIEGO, CALIFORNIA
7 MOVES

Don't worry about the boxes, the house, the furniture, or the paint job. Just worry about helping your kids find friends.

—*JULIE*
SAN FRANCISCO, CALIFORNIA
5 MOVES

I GOT INVOLVED IN EVERYTHING MY KIDS DID in the new town. This way, my kids knew how much I cared for them, and I got to network with other Moms soon after the move.

—*P.M.*
TULSA, OKLAHOMA
8 MOVES

“Move on a weekend. Have the kids spend a special last sleepover at their friends' houses, and enjoy the day. It's fun for the kids, and what a relief for the parents!”

—*CeeCee*
RENO, NEVADA
5 MOVES

FIND SOMETHING YOUR KID LIKES in the new place. The fact that my daughter liked the curtains between the dining room and the living room—like in a theater—became the central feature of why she was moving here.

—*NANCY*
PORTLAND, MAINE
8 MOVES

WE HAD OUR KIDS GO AROUND with colored duct tape and markers and label the boxes. They devised a system where things were color-coded and labeled by room, along with a general list of what was in the boxes. It made them feel important and helpful. And it wasn't just an act of mercy on our part; they really WERE helpful! The movers easily put the boxes in the right rooms, and we knew which ones were the highest priority to unpack.

> —*MARTY*
> *CHICAGO, ILLINOIS*
> *8 MOVES*

. . . .

LET LITTLE KIDS UNPACK THEIR TOYS right away. Don't even take out the toilet paper before you take their toys out of the boxes. I have seen this work wonders with friends of mine. Moving is a big scary thing for little kids and having a familiar toy in their hand right away can make a big difference.

> —*BOB SCHULTZ*
> *HOPEWELL TOWNSHIP, PENNSYLVANIA*
> *2 MOVES*

. . . .

YOU NEVER KNOW HOW YOUR KIDS' new friends might help you out. When we moved, our daughter was in school, but we couldn't find a daycare for our younger son for weeks. Then, my daughter made friends with a girl in her class, and her parents—who also had a daughter that was our son's age—immediately found a place for us at this exclusive daycare center which their daughter attended. Our daycare problem was solved, thanks to people we had just met!

> —*JWAIII*
> *ATLANTA, GEORGIA*
> *15 MOVES*

WHEN YOU'RE GOING TO MOVE from place to place with kids, give them a backpack and tell them, "Whatever you want to take needs to go in there." That way, it's not you deciding what toys they want to take; it's them. You explain to them that everything else is going to be carted up, and for the next 30 days or so, they're not going to have other toys.

—THOMAS M.W. "MIKE" DOWNS
SYRACUSE, NEW YORK
21 MOVES

• • • • • • • •

WHEN MOVING WITH CHILDREN, encourage them to be creative in meeting new friends. We moved when one of my daughters was in the fourth grade and she got a list of all the neighborhood's fourth graders and sent them letters saying, "Would you be my friend?" One of the little girls said, "I already have a lot of friends, but you can never have too many."

—S.F.
SAN ANTONIO, TEXAS
8 MOVES

• • • • • • • •

PICKING OUT PAINT COLORS FOR THE NEW HOUSE is an important task. You need to paint a really big swatch and hold it up in the light before you can be sure about the shade. We had our older kids paint some shades we were considering onto big cardboard pieces. We just spread out big sheets underneath for the clean up. And it didn't matter if the painting wasn't perfect. It saved us time, was fun for them, and helped us finalize our color choices.

—C.H.
LOS ANGELES, CALIFORNIA
6 MOVES

DON'T BE OVERPROTECTIVE and think you need to coddle your kids. You could end up doing more damage than good. For an older kid, being walked into school by Mommy can lead to a lot of teasing and make it harder for them to integrate well.

—*MISSY*
DETROIT, MICHIGAN
*10 MOVES*

• • • • • • • •

BECAUSE A MOVE IS A SCARY THING for little kids, try to make it as exciting as possible for them. Let them help decorate their new room and pick out the colors for the walls. Try to get them to see it not as a big change but as an exciting adventure to a new place. Point out all the good stuff about the new town. Take them to the park near your home. Don't dwell on the stuff that was in your old town.

—*ANONYMOUS*
SOUTH BEND, INDIANA
2 MOVES

• • • • • • • •

GIVE YOUR KIDS STRUCTURE as soon as possible. When we moved from suburbia to an intown location with our two kids, one of the first things we did—accidentally, actually—was find our "hangout restaurant," the place we could turn to whenever there were no other options. The biggest benefit of the restaurant, aside from the good pizza and beer, was that the kids found a place they would be comfortable with. Every time we'd pass by, they'd point it out. It helped them feel like part of the neighborhood.

—*JWAIII*
ATLANTA, GEORGIA
15 MOVES

A walk through your old house and neighborhood will allow a child to say goodbye to favorite things. Pictures, videos, and other reminders can help, too.

—*PEDIATRICS HEALTH MONITOR*

WE LET OUR SON HAVE HIS PICK OF BEDROOMS in the new house. At first I don't think he believed us. He was very excited when he told family about "his" room. We also let him have a say in how the room was decorated. It was still hard on him, but I think these things helped.

—*WALTER HUGHES*
CLEVELAND, OHIO
7 MOVES

• • • • • • • • •

TO HELP CHILDREN ADJUST TO MOVING, take them around to meet all the neighbors. From the time my son was very small, we went to church immediately after moving and I told him to introduce himself to all the kids his age. I taught him how to give a strong handshake.

—*NANCY*
NICEVILLE, FLORIDA
8 MOVES

• • • • • • • • •

IN ORDER TO EASE MY SON INTO THE MOVE and change of schools, I made an appointment with the new school and arranged for him to spend an entire day there, meeting new teachers and classmates. I timed the move so that I wouldn't have to pull him out of school mid-year. I also put him in summer camp so that he would make friends and adjust to the new neighborhood before the new school year started.

—*J.L.*
CHICAGO, ILLINOIS
3 MOVES

Go Dog, Go: How to Move Your Pets

If there's one thing that can be more stressful than moving all your worldly belongings and your kids, it's moving your pets. After all, you can't explain to Kitty how she's really going to like the new litter box—especially when the litter box is located in completely unfamiliar territory that has yet to be "marked." And that's assuming Kitty, or your dog, fish, bird or iguana, survives the dreaded drive to the unfamiliar place. How do you accomplish the purrrfect move? Some say tranquilizers help (for your pet, not you). Read on.

IF YOU HAVE TO MOVE FISH, put the bags in a cheap Styrofoam cooler. That way, if the bags leak or break, you don't end up with a wet cardboard box and dead fish.

—KIM JAFFE
REDMOND, WASHINGTON
6 MOVES

THERE'S NO WAY YOU'RE GETTING THAT CAT INTO A BOX.

—W. BRUCE CAMERON
SANTA MONICA, CALIFORNIA
12 MOVES

I USUALLY MOVE MY PETS LAST, putting them in their carriers for the ride over. I keep the cats inside for the first week or two so they don't run away. When I moved across the country it was a cold winter. Two of the cats rode in the back of my pickup truck with little hand warmers under the covers to keep them toasty. My elderly cat couldn't stay warm that way, though, so she rode on my lap for three days.

—*J.A.*
DURHAM, NORTH CAROLINA
16 MOVES

TRY NOT TO ALTER YOUR DOG'S DIET during the move and definitely do not feed it rawhide treats on an eight-hour car ride. I forgot food for our dog, so I kept feeding her treats. When we got to the new house, there was diarrhea all over the kennel. The first night we were there, the dog vomited all over the new carpet.

—*WADE*
AURORA, ILLINOIS
5 MOVES

CATS DON'T LIKE TO MOVE. When we moved into our new house, first I moved all her things and a blanket she liked to the new house. When I got her there, I put those things in a room—the one farthest away from any outside doors—and locked her in there for 24 hours to give her a chance to calm down and get used to the new place.

—*LYNN JONES*
KIRKLAND, WASHINGTON
6 MOVES

ALWAYS KEEP ANIMALS IN A CONTAINER when you move. One time I was moving my brother's cat without one, and the cat was so freaked out that it peed all over the car. You can never get that smell out. We've steam cleaned it a couple times, but it still smells back there.

—*JOE*
MILWAUKEE, WISCONSIN
8 MOVES

• • • • • • • •

"Feeding the cat a sliver of Dramamine prior to the car ride might work—as long as she doesn't immediately throw up that very sliver of Dramamine."

—*MARSHALL MILLER*
ALBANY, NEW YORK
11 MOVES

• • • • • • • •

THERE IS NO WAY TO MOVE CATS without getting a lot of "cat-titude." You aren't even allowed to sedate them when they fly now! Our cats were pretty unhappy when my husband got them off the plane. They hid on top of the kitchen cabinets for a day and didn't eat.

—*ANONYMOUS*
GOLDEN, COLORADO
25 MOVES

WE MOVED TWO DOGS, two cats and a hedgehog. The hardest part about traveling with pets was the motels along the way. Most take a dog or two but almost none take as many animals as we had. We snuck them into motels—once by taking off the screen of the motel room window and slipping them in across a flower bed.

> —C. HOPE CLARK
> PHOENIX, ARIZONA
> 8 MOVES

Take one room, put your pets inside, and close the door. Leave lots of their favorite toys inside, and come visit them every hour.

—JOHN PLATT
SOMERSET,
NEW JERSEY
4 MOVES

• • • • • • • •

I HAD TO PUT MY PUPPY IN A CARRY CAB. I had her in the front seat with me, but she was so scared of all the noise that she wept and scratched for hours. I had to put a blanket over the cab, talk to her in a loving voice. I told her everything was going to be OK.

> —ANGELIQUE S.
> SYRACUSE, NEW YORK
> 5 MOVES

• • • • • • • •

WE MOVED TWO CATS BY AIR. We were able to buy the middle seat in a row of three, and the larger cat, a 15-pound Maine Coon, rode there in her carrier, with the top open, much to the amusement of passengers passing in the aisle. Fortunately there were no allergic types nearby, and the cabin crew didn't hassle us.

> —FARRON D. BROUGHER
> ANAHEIM, CALIFORNIA
> 4 MOVES

• • • • • • • •

MOVE HALF YOUR FURNITURE into the new house before you bring your cats inside. You never want to move your cats into an empty house. They need some of their stuff around that smells like them.

> —MARGARET C.
> AUSTIN, TEXAS

WHEN YOU ACTUALLY GET TO YOUR NEW HOME, be
sure that you confine your cat to one room and
allow her to become comfortable in her new
surroundings before she is allowed out in the rest
of the home. Just be sure that you don't make the
mistake of choosing a room that had obviously
been inhabited by another cat who "acted out"—
this will not do anything to put your cat at ease.

> —C. HUTCHINS
> BARLING, ARKANSAS
> 4 MOVES

• • • • • • • •

WE JUST MOVED THREE CATS IN A CAR, taking
turns trying to keep them out of the driver's lap.
They had a decent setup, all things considered.
They had their own food and water bowls on the
floor behind the driver's seat, and a litter box on
the floor behind the passenger's seat. But I
swear, I must have vacuumed 15 pounds of cat
litter out of that car by the end of the trip, and
we only started with a 10 pound bag.

> —JOHN RODGERS
> SEATTLE, WASHINGTON
> 6 MOVES

• • • • • • • •

SOME FRIENDS OF MINE RENTED AN APARTMENT and
asked their landlord if they could pay a reduced
fee for the first month. They had a dog and
wanted their pet to adjust to the new surroundings over a longer period of time. Because they
were not at the apartment full time, the landlord
agreed to the terms and reduced the first month's
rent. They would spend random weekends and
some weeknights at the place with the dog,
making him comfortable by the time they actually
made the full move.

> —M.B.
> NEW YORK, NEW YORK
> 3 MOVES

HEAVEN SCENT: FROM ONE CAT PERSON TO ANOTHER

Cats are creatures of habit that really like things to be exactly the same way every day. A move is traumatic for them. Often, cats will become so panicked in a new house they'll hide so well that their owners have a hard time finding them. This can be traumatic for the owner, too!

As you start packing, put your cat in one room, preferably a room the cat likes. Keep that room as intact as possible for as long as possible. Put something soft like a blanket or towel in the room for the cat to sleep on.

On moving day, take the cat over first. Set up one room in your new home and put the cat in it, with the blanket or towel that's now covered with her scent. Close the door so the cat can't get out! Turn on some white noise, such as a TV or radio, to cover up the noise of moving elsewhere in the house.

During the move, check on kitty every few hours, petting and reassuring her. After you're moved in, take the cat out of the room and carry her around the new house. Put her back in the room. Later, let her roam around the house, supervised. Once she seems comfortable, give her the roam of the house.

—*S.W., VETERINARIAN*
LEHIGH VALLEY, PENNSYLVANIA
8 MOVES

WE HAVE THREE CATS. There's no easy way to move them, but the last time we did, we had overlapping leases, so we left them at the old house until we were just about done there and then brought them to the new one. That way they weren't alone in a new house while we were finishing up at the old one.

—*BRAD COOK*
CHICO, CALIFORNIA
6 MOVES

• • • • • • • •

I HAVE A RABBIT AND AN IGUANA. We moved them last. For those types of animals, stress can kill them. Try not to move things out of their general area till the last minute, to avoid them being anxious. And don't forget to love them and let them know you're still around.

—*RITA PORTER*
SPRINGFIELD, MISSOURI
7 MOVES

• • • • • • • •

WE TAKE OUR ANIMALS OVER A WEEK PRIOR to the move and let them get used to the place. The cat roams around the empty house, and we take our dogs on a walk through the new neighborhood. This eases the anxiety of transition for the animal.

—*LENNARD HAYNES SR.*
HOUSTON, TEXAS
6 MOVES

• • • • • • • •

GATSBY FREAKED OUT OVER A MOVE so badly that he ripped off the door of the plastic carrier while I was transporting him and bolted down the street. I did catch him, but he howled every night for a couple weeks until he got used to the new place.

—*ANONYMOUS*
NEW YORK, NEW YORK
10 MOVES

Pets allowed to fly in airline cabins: dogs, cats, birds, ferrets, rabbits, hamsters and guinea pigs. Not allowed: monkeys, pot-bellied pigs, reptiles, frogs, mice, rats, and spiders.

—*DELTA AIRLINES*

THE BEST WAY TO PACK A CAT is to use an oversized carrier, like a crate made for a puppy, with a shoebox for a litter box. The cat is confined but still has room to move around and go to the bathroom if necessary.

—*JOY FODER*
FAIRFAX, VIRGINIA
3 MOVES

. . . .

"Do not let a dog run into a new home—the chances of him or her not marking territory is slim."

—*VANESSA WILKINSON*
COLORA, MARYLAND
6 MOVES

. . . .

I TRAVELED WITH OUR TWO CATS alone while towing a U-Haul trailer. I thought I would make them "comfortable," so I bought a dog gate for the back compartment of my SUV, put out a bowl of food, a bowl of water, a litter pan, and let the cats back there free. Big mistake. As I was pulling out of my driveway I hit the brakes pretty hard. Of course, the water spilled, the food and litter dumped, and the cats started yelping. One cat sat in the wet litter for the next 8 hours without moving, and the other crawled under the seats, under the pedals, and did not stay in the back. It was not a fun drive.

—*MARC CLAYBON*
DENVER, COLORADO

EXPECT SURPRISES WHEN MOVING WITH PETS. Even though Greta, our dog, was fully housebroken before we moved, she had "accidents" for a time after my fiancé and I moved into our apartment. Maybe she was under more stress than we realized. In any case, we had to re-potty train her, keeping her in the kitchen for a while, before we let her have the run of the first floor.

> —*JENNIFER K.*
> *SHEBOYGON, WISCONSIN*
> 🚚 *3 MOVES*

• • • • • • • •

IF YOU HAVE A BIRD, check the cage before you move. Everything was out of my apartment except for the cockatiel. The entire place was clean. I was taking the cage out, and it fell apart and down the stairs. Bird poop and water and colored seed flew all the way down to my front door. And he got out, so I had to keep going back to the apartment for three days to catch him.

> —*BONNIE NAUMANN*
> *HOLMES, NEW YORK*

• • • • • • • •

DRIVING HALF-WAY ACROSS THE COUNTRY with a dog who doesn't like to go to the bathroom in public was fun. We tried to stop every two or three hours and walk him behind a gas station so nobody could see him pee. For some reason, it helped him feel more comfortable when my husband and I stayed out of the car for an extended period of time, like to get something to eat. But if it was a quick stop, just to get gas or something, he acted incredibly shy.

> —*S.A.*
> *LAKE FOREST, CALIFORNIA*
> 🚚 *8 MOVES*

I let my dog into the new place and let her sniff to her heart's content.

> —*CELIA DUNBAR*
> *OKLAHOMA CITY, OKLAHOMA*
> 🚚 *23 MOVES*

I TREATED MY CAT SORT OF LIKE A ROOMMATE.
He stayed with me all through the move. Anytime I
went to and from the new place, he rode along. I
think these little visits helped him get familiar with
the new place before we made the final trip.

—JEFF ELLIS
CROSS LANES, WEST VIRGINIA
7 MOVES

• • • • • • • •

FIND A SAFE PLACE FOR YOUR PETS. Moving day
was stressful for our dog. He wanted to be
everywhere, watching everything. So we tied
him with a long leash inside our garage and
left the garage door opened. That way, he
could watch us going in and out of the house,
yet he wasn't outside in the hot sun and he
couldn't run away or get stepped on.

—MOLLY BROWN
ALLENTOWN, PENNSYLVANIA
4 MOVES

• • • • • • • •

I HAVE THREE CATS, and I drove them out to
Kansas from Colorado by myself. I put them in
crates, and I made sure to stop every couple of
hours, open their cages, pet them, give them a
sip of water and make sure they were OK. I didn't
feed them anything during the drive because
I didn't want them to get sick. I would also
recommend having music on—it seems to
calm them.

—CANDICE PORTER
OVERLAND PARK, KANSAS
5 MOVES

I HAVE A CAT THAT WAS 12 YEARS OLD at the time
of this last move. I boarded him while the movers
were packing my space to lessen his anxiety, and
had the vet administer some kitty valium before I
picked him up. I also made certain that there was
a place in my new home that he could call his
own while adjusting. He stayed in the hall closet
for two weeks after we moved!

—*LIZ SCHERER*
ANNAPOLIS, MARYLAND
3 MOVES

" **What does one do with the
family goldfish? We took ours
along in a big garbage can filled
halfway with water. The fish
made it!** "

—*CLAUDE GRUENER*
AUSTIN, TEXAS
4 MOVES

I HAD A LOVELY CAT NAMED HEMINGWAY.
Unfortunately, I moved to an apartment complex that did not accept animals, and I had
to put him up for adoption. My real estate
broker adopted him and Hemingway was
very lucky. If you have an animal, seek a
place where he/she is welcome. If you can't
find such a place, think ahead and find your
animal a good home.

—*MINDY PHILLIPS LAWRENCE*
FARMINGTON, MISSOURI
8 MOVES

A health
certificate is
required when
shipping your
pet as air
cargo. The
certificate
may also be
required by
the state
you're
traveling to.

—*Delta Airlines*

I ONCE TRIED TO MOVE A CAT, and when we got to the new house it ran up the chimney and got into the walls. The next time I moved that particular cat, I got the house together first, then moved the cat and locked it in the bathroom until it calmed down.

> —*Hania*
> *Seattle, Washington*
> *8 moves*

• • • • • • • •

I HAVE CATS AND I GIVE THEM BOXES to play in while I'm packing/unpacking. I let them roam the car during the drives because they hate being locked in their carriers. And I give them tuna treats when we get settled in the new place.

> —*Sarah Clark*
> *New York, New York*
> *9 moves*

Help! Professional Movers vs. Inexpensive Friends

Two roads diverged in a wood . . . but both of these roads are pretty well traveled. The dilemma is: Do you use an experienced crew of professional movers, whom you've never met, and trust them with your most valuable items at an hourly rate? Or do you use friends who may be cheap but, uh, slightly less motivated (not to mention uninsured)? Both have their upsides and downsides. Here are some stories and tips to help you make sure the road you choose is decidedly smooth.

PAY SOMEONE TO DO IT; don't let friends do it for free. When you are paying someone, you have the right to boss them around and have high expectations. Believe me, it is worth it, because you can't really get mad at someone who is working for free.

—ERIKA
NEW YORK, NEW YORK
2 MOVES

MOVERS BREAK THINGS— PRECIOUS THINGS.

—JANE POWELL
EARLYSVILLE, VIRGINIA
20 MOVES

Moving develops male camaraderie.

—*Daniel M.*
Toronto,
Ontario, Canada
🚚 *3 moves*

CONSIDER PAYING SOMEONE to come in and wrap up the stuff that's most valuable to you, even if you can't afford to hire professional movers. You can save a lot of money this way AND protect the items you care most about. Professional packers have been trained to wrap things up the right way, which is particularly important when you cram everything into the back of a U-Haul.

—*JOAN K. HITCHENS*
CENTENNIAL, COLORADO
🚚 *3 MOVES*

• • • • • • • •

NOTHING MOTIVATES PEOPLE to help you move more than food. The underlying sentiment you should convey to friends who help you is gratitude. I like to move first thing in the morning. If you're going to ask someone to be at your home at 7 a.m., you should have breakfast waiting for them. And if you have a lot of things to move, give them pizza for lunch, too.

—*C.S.*
VIRGINIA BEACH, VIRGINIA
🚚 *4 MOVES*

• • • • • • • •

OUR MOVING COMPANY TOOK EVERYTHING OUT of the old house and had it all arranged in the new house BEFORE we arrived. OK, we did some re-arranging later. But our beds were assembled and made, the kitchen was stocked, the dishes were arranged, and all the utilities were working when we first stepped in the house! It really took a lot of the stress out of moving to a new house.

—*E.G.*
NEW HAVEN, CONNECTICUT
🚚 *3 MOVES*

DO IT ALL YOURSELF. I think it is a lazy thing to hire people. If you need some extra hands, then get some friends to come over. It will be a fun, bonding experience. It has always seemed like a waste of money to get someone else to do your moving for you—after all, who will be nicer to your stuff than YOU?

—*ALME BLAIR*
NEW YORK, NEW YORK
4 MOVES

• • • • • • • •

" Hire movers! Friends are great, but they take forever, and a couple kegs to boot. "

—*JEANNE ECKMAN*
LANCASTER, PENNSYLVANIA
2 MOVES

• • • • • • • •

I THINK IT'S AN UNWRITTEN RULE that at age 35 you should just suck it up and hire a mover. At this point, you are past the days of getting friends to help and then buying them beer and pizza when it's all done. If you're 35 or older, don't cheap out by not hiring professional help.

—*BOB SUSNJARA*
ARLINGTON HEIGHTS, ILLINOIS
5 MOVES

• • • • • • • •

I SAVED ALL MY CHANGE FOR A YEAR to pay my movers and it was worth every penny. You don't have to worry about doing it yourself or the hassle of asking your friends. They were pros and it was a piece of cake.

—*P.G.*
SAN ANTONIO, TEXAS
25 MOVES

TIPS FOR HIRING MOVERS

GET SEVERAL ESTIMATES AND GO WITH A FIXED ESTIMATE wherever possible. Check out the company's record with the Better Business Bureau. How many complaints have they had? Were they resolved amicably? The lowest price is not always the best service. Look for hidden charges, like insurance, travel, tolls and gas. Make sure there are enough guys—too few will up the costs considerably.

> —*LIZ SCHERER*
> *ANNAPOLIS, MARYLAND*
> *3 MOVES*

• • • • • • • •

BEWARE OF HIDDEN CHARGES with moving companies. I once hired people to move a piano from a third floor apartment and it ended up costing me $400 extra because the workers had to disassemble the hallway and staircase since the piano couldn't be taken apart and they were charging me by the hour.

> —*MARK FAIWELL*
> *BUFFALO GROVE, ILLINOIS*
> *4 MOVES*

• • • • • • • • •

CHECK TO MAKE SURE MOVERS HAVE INSURANCE. Then, if something gets damaged, it's covered.

> —*SAMANTHA*
> *LOS ANGELES, CALIFORNIA*
> *6 MOVES*

IF YOU'RE HANDING YOUR BOXES OVER to a mover, count the total number of boxes and label them as such (box 1 of 30, 2 of 30, etc.) Keep a running list of what's in each box so if something gets lost, you'll know what's missing and what to claim on your insurance.

—*SUSAN*
WESTFIELD, NEW JERSEY
5 MOVES

● ● ● ● ● ● ● ●

THE GREATEST THING ABOUT PROFESSIONAL movers is that you just stay out of their way and let them do their jobs. They know what they're doing. I pack valuables myself and take them with me because there have been times irreplaceable valuables have been misplaced or stolen. If you would rather the movers pack everything, photograph valuables before the move and make sure there is a time/date stamp on the photo. It's easier to prove theft if you have evidence.

—*J. M. CORNWELL*
TABERNASH, COLORADO
11 MOVES

● ● ● ● ● ● ● ●

IF YOU'RE YOUNG, YOU CAN MOVE YOURSELF. But the older we all get the worse I feel about asking friends for their help. It really gets to be a drag, and none of us are in shape to do that anymore. It really is quite a physical workout to move all that heavy stuff.

—*DAN SANTOS*
GREENTREE, PENNSYLVANIA
5 MOVES

Danger! Movers won't transport common hazardous materials like paint thinners, oils, varnishes, firearms and ammunition, propane, motor fuels and oils, nail polish remover, bleach and aerosol cans.

—*MOVING.COM*

I OFFERED THE MOVERS the leftover booze in my fridge and they loved it. It was 8:30 a.m.! Movers will drink and eat everything in your fridge . . . so don't worry about clearing that out before they start working.

—*AL*
TORONTO, ONTARIO, CANADA
6 MOVES

• • • • • • • •

" Never ask movers to rearrange furniture more than once. Payback in thievery or broken items often makes the first arrangement look pretty darn good. "

—*CASSANDRA FOX*
FAIRFAX STATION, VIRGINIA

• • • • • • • •

HIRE HELP. No joke. When you roll off your mattress onto the floor on the first morning in your new apartment, you will feel a large, searing object akin to a frozen ice pick moving quickly through your back. The costs of removing that ice pick with massage, bathing and acupuncture will exceed that of Jim and Tony's vans.

—*NICHOLAS SCHIFRIN*
NEW YORK, NEW YORK

IF YOU HAVE TO RELOCATE FOR WORK, ask the new company if they would consider paying for your move. If you don't ask, they probably aren't going to offer.

—*ANONYMOUS*
READING, PENNSYLVANIA
 *4 MOVES*

• • • • • • • •

WHEN I MOVED APARTMENTS, I got moving insurance. It was the best decision of my life. The moving guys say that they will take responsibility for your items, but when push came to shove (and they dropped my piano and broke it) I ended up being very happy I had sprung for the extra insurance.

—*DAVID KARL*

• • • • • • • •

IF YOUR FRIENDS ARE HELPING YOU MOVE, have everything in boxes before they get there. Your friends love you, but no one wants to watch you throw your underwear into bags.

—*APRIL SMITH*
BOSTON, MASSACHUSETTS

• • • • • • • •

PAY FOR HELP. Sure it's easy to agonize over a few hundred dollars, but break a few items or your back and the money looks like a good deal.

—*JASON WAXMAN*

Last week I helped my friend stay put. It's a lot easier than helping someone move. I just went over to his house and made sure he did not start to load sh*t into a truck.

—*MITCH HEDBERG*
COMEDIAN

MOVERS: THE HORROR STORY

MOVERS LOVE TO TAKE THEIR TIME BECAUSE THEY GET PAID—quite generously, I might add—by the hour. Our movers were two pot-bellied, potty-mouthed and gruff fellows. Even though we helped move a lot of boxes to speed the process, it took close to 10 hours anyway.

> —*MICHELE HENRY*
> *TORONTO, ONTARIO, CANADA*
> *3 MOVES*

• • • • • • • • •

WHEN OUR MOVERS ARRIVED, you could feel the vibrations from the loud music. It was a bunch of kids, and they were running around with our furniture. It was bad. Even our real estate agent was cringing.

> —*LOIS GREEN*
> *COLUMBIA, SOUTH CAROLINA*
> *5 MOVES*

• • • • • • • • •

MOVERS ARE EXTORTIONISTS. I tipped everybody $50 each, and the guys said to me, "That's all?" I said, "I don't have any more cash." And he said, "You could write a check." So I gave them all $100. What could I do? They knew where I lived.

> —*CHRISTINE BEIDEL*
> *RUTHERFORD, NEW JERSEY*
> *2 MOVES*

DON'T ASK MOVERS TO DO THE IMPOSSIBLE. We recently moved to a high-rise apartment building, and we had this big chest with bookshelves. They couldn't get it in the elevator, so I had them take it to storage. The manager said it was just as well. He said one time they had a woman with a king-size sleeper sofa that wouldn't fit in the elevator. She made them take it up the stairs. The movers got to the 3rd- or 4th-floor landing and walked back down empty handed. They asked the manager, "Do you know where we work?" "Yes," he said. They said: "Well, you can call our boss and tell him that we quit." And they walked out.

> —*CAROLINE ELEDGE*
> *KANSAS CITY, MISSOURI*
> 14 MOVES

• • • • • • • • •

STATE THE OBVIOUS so that your belongings are handled with as much care as you would handle them. When our son was in 2nd grade we built this 3-foot long dinosaur out of papier-mâché and attached it to a plywood base. The movers just used a big box and dropped it to the bottom and piled all kinds of other stuff on top of it. It was something you can't replace.

> —*WADE*
> *AURORA, ILLINOIS*
> 5 MOVES

SAN JOSE, CALIFORNIA

IF SOMETHING SOUNDS TOO GOOD TO BE TRUE, it probably is, and you may end up getting swindled. My husband and I boxed ourselves and hired shady, inexpensive movers to move us from Manhattan to Brooklyn. They estimated the job would take 4 hours; it took more than 12. We got billed for the overtime and spent our first night in the new apartment writing apology notes to our co-op board, which was none-too-impressed with our rude and inconsiderate movers. Had we hired reputable, more "expensive" movers, we would have saved a ton of dough—and had a much less stressful day.

—SASHA EMMONS
BROOKLYN, NEW YORK
7 MOVES

. . . .

JUST REMEMBER, using friends might be inexpensive, but you also have to realize that you will be moving these same friends sometime in the next year. They help you, you help them. By using their services this Saturday, one of your Saturdays in the near future has just been scheduled for you. So, it's not exactly equal to the cost of pizza.

—JWAIII
ATLANTA, GEORGIA
15 MOVES

. . . .

I HAVE MOVED FIVE TIMES and helped countless other people move. The best thing I ever did was to hire movers. Expensive—yes, but watching other people move my things while it rained outside was some of the best money I've ever spent.

—MITCH S.
CHICAGO, ILLINOIS
5 MOVES

Sure, they say a rental truck is "$9.99" but that is a "LIE." They charge so much per mile it's crazy. Our $9.99 rental turned into $125.00.

—CRYSTAL BAHMAIE
BROOKLYN,
NEW YORK
6 MOVES

IF YOU DON'T HIRE PROFESSIONAL MOVERS then you have to understand that some of your stuff is going to get broken. There are no two ways about it. I'm not saying that you should use professionals —because it does cost lots of money—but if you don't you can say goodbye to some of your stuff because it's going to get dropped and break.

—*CHARLENE DEPASQUALE*
PITTSBURGH, PENNSYLVANIA
2 MOVES

• • • • • • • •

If you help me move, I'll supply a case of beer. A cheap pack, though. Not import. Bud Light. Plus pizza.

—*JENNY DISALVO*
BOSTON, MASSACHUSETTS
8 MOVES

• • • • • • • •

DO YOUR HOMEWORK ABOUT YOUR MOVERS. The strangest feeling comes from when you receive the docket from the movers, giving you a list of boxes, furniture, and other things that they have counted and then watching them drive away with everything that you own. All you have is a piece of paper in your hand. You paid them to take it all. You have to trust that the company that you employed is honest, trustworthy and in the end, you will get all your valued possessions when you reach your final destination.

—*MARIE*
SYDNEY, AUSTRALIA
3 MOVES

THE PLUSES OF HIRING MOVERS: they showed up when they were supposed to and they were able to get my couch out the window when it didn't fit through the door. The only con was that they broke a glass frame and wouldn't take responsibility. Also, they sent two trucks by mistake.

> —JOELLE SELLNER
> LOS ANGELES, CALIFORNIA
> 8 MOVES

• • • • • • • •

ONCE YOU ARE OUT OF COLLEGE, there is no excuse for forcing your friends and family to carry your stuff up and down multiple flights of stairs.

> —L.K.
> NEW YORK, NEW YORK
> 5 MOVES

• • • • • • • •

BE READY FOR THE MOVERS. A lot of people think that hiring movers makes moving effortless. Not really! When they arrive, movers descend upon your home, split up into different rooms, and pack quicker than you could ever imagine. I've heard of movers who packed two shoes from a pair in two different boxes because the shoes were in different rooms! I've also heard of movers who packed trash right in its trashcan! Have things clean and ready ahead of time.

> —ELLEN
> PITTSBURGH, PENNSYLVANIA
> 11 MOVES

• • • • • • • •

TIP YOUR MOVERS. Those guys are getting paid $10, $12 an hour. It's nice to be appreciated. Buy them lunch, offer them something to eat or drink. The more they think you respect them, the more they're going to respect your stuff.

> —JOE
> MILWAUKEE, WISCONSIN
> 8 MOVES

Shipping your motorcycle? Use only licensed and insured transporters. Carriers and brokers should be able to provide a copy of their license and a "Certificate of Insurance."

—MOVING.COM

ENOUGH TO MAKE YOU SEASICK

When you move overseas, the moving company puts your entire life in a big container, and it takes 6-8 weeks to ship. These containers are stacked onto cargo ships and then sail to your selected destination. Just like the airlines, these containers sometimes get "lost."

As we stayed in temporary lodging in Germany waiting for our couches and bookcases and tables to arrive, I checked with the moving company to see how often these containers go missing. Their answer: "Oh, pretty often." They explained that these containers get stacked really high on the ship, but they can't lock them down because  they are so heavy they could actually make the ship flip over in turbulent waters. At any given time, there are apparently thousands of these containers floating in the ocean that have fallen off ships in transit, and are too heavy and too dangerous to retrieve. Eight weeks later, when our "container" arrived, I was extremely grateful and to this day have a new appreciation for the entire moving process.

—SCOTT A. MOORE
EISLEBEN, GERMANY
10 MOVES

CONVINCE THE FRIENDS THAT you are leaving soon that the only way they can spend quality time with you before you go is if they help you pack.

—*MEREDITH*
NEW YORK, NEW YORK
3 MOVES

• • • • • • • •

IF YOU CAN AFFORD TO HIRE MOVERS, do it. When my husband and I were dating, he moved to West Palm Beach, and he decided to do it himself. The truck he rented smelled like cigarettes and caused me to have an allergic reaction. After driving 11 hours—sneezing and miserable—from Atlanta to West Palm Beach, we started to unload the furniture. Of course nothing in the truck was loaded in any kind of real order so it meant taking stuff out to unload other stuff, putting it back in the truck and going back and forth from his tiny, garage apartment to the storage facility.

—*K.S.*
PALM BEACH GARDENS, FLORIDA

• • • • • • • •

BUY FOOD AND DRINKS—beer, I mean—and guys will show up to help.

—*PATRICIA WHIPPLE*
CHARLEVOIX, MICHIGAN

• • • • • • • •

IF YOU WANT TO KEEP TRACK OF SOMETHING, put it in the refrigerator. Movers will not snatch it from there. Car keys, bills to pay, little Billy's favorite stuffed animal, directions to the new school—they all go in the refrigerator.

—*NAN ANDREWS AMISH*
EL GRANADA, CALIFORNIA
10 MOVES

OUR MOVES HAVE BEEN CORPORATE MOVES and we always have a company come in and pack it up, load it up, haul it, unload it. Pro: It is much quicker and easier than doing it yourself. Con: It's not their stuff, so it's not wrapped with as much TLC as if you were doing it.

—*TINA MUSIAL*
MATAWAN, NEW JERSEY
6 *MOVES*

. . . .

JUST DON'T TRY TO DO IT ALL ON YOUR OWN. I am a single mother, and I've made this mistake over and over. I think the kids and I can handle it, then moving day comes and it's overwhelming and awful. Now I make sure I have friends lined up, or my older kids around, or a hire mover.

—*SUSANNA RODELL*
CHARLESTON, WEST VIRGINIA
LITERALLY LOST COUNT

. . . .

MOVING SUCKS. My friends think that because I'm built and athletic, I like to move. All I want to say is: Hire movers, that's their job, not mine.

—*C.F.*
LIBERTYVILLE, ILLINOIS
8 *MOVES*

. . . .

USE YOUR SEX TO YOUR ADVANTAGE. I just bat my eyelashes at guys I know and say, "I have to move Saturday . . ."

—*K.K.*
PHILADELPHIA, PENNSYLVANIA
7 *MOVES*

HELL ON WHEELS

WHEN YOU DECIDE TO MOVE CROSS-COUNTRY, you may not realize the importance of finding a reputable company to transport your car. The company I hired to ship my car from New York to Los Angeles promised to get the job done in two to three weeks. Instead, my car sat in a New Jersey lot for more than a month. My parents had to track down the car and, essentially, kidnap it from the transport company. The company's explanation was that it doesn't ship cars on half-empty flatbeds. The truck had to be filled before it would make the cross-country trip. This crucial tidbit was apparently buried in the fine print.

> —*HEATHER*
> *MARINA DEL REY, CALIFORNIA*
> 🚚 *3 MOVES*

• • • • • • • • •

WHEN MY FAMILY MOVED FROM CALIFORNIA to the Midwest, we had our vehicles transported by a company that specialized in moving cars to shooting locations for the movie industry. It was much less expensive than the commercial moving companies.

> —*C.F.*
> *IOWA CITY, IOWA*
> 🚚 *15 MOVES*

• • • • • • • • •

BE PREPARED FOR A CHALLENGE if you have to ship your car. I met a lady who had shipped her car three times with the same company, and she recommended them. My car arrived on the west coast, safe and sound. The problem was, it arrived three weeks after I was hoping it would! I incurred $650 in car rental fees that I wasn't expecting.

> —*LAURA VINCENT*
> *NOVATO, CALIFORNIA*
> 🚚 *2 MOVES*

YOU SHOULD NOT MOVE BOXES if you're a girl. Hire somebody to do it for you; it's not worth it to save a few dollars.

> —*HELEN KURTZ*
> *MINNEAPOLIS, MINNESOTA*
> *4 MOVES*

IF YOU'RE TEMPTED TO HIRE TEENAGERS or other inexpensive but inexperienced movers, hire them to UNPACK your U-Haul. Hire professionals to PACK the truck if you don't want everything to be a broken mess when you arrive.

> —*MARSHALL MILLER*
> *ALBANY, NEW YORK*
> *11 MOVES*

I'VE HAD TO MOVE EVERY YEAR for the past 5 years, and the best thing that I've learned is to "conveniently" leave town right around moving time and make your boyfriend do it. Last year I went to Australia and my boyfriend had to move for me. This year I will be in Florida! Second option: Develop arthritis and your wrists won't be able to carry much, meaning once again the ol' boyfriend will have to step in.

> —*ALLISON BROWNLEE*
> *BOULDER, COLORADO*
> *5 MOVES*

You might be able to negotiate a better price with movers if you move during the off-season or during the week, when they are not as busy.

—*THE EVERYTHING HOMESELLING BOOK*

STICK CLOSE TO YOUR MOVERS. I was really comforted by being involved with every step of the packing. I've moved so many times and learned that even if you hire large movers who pack everything and ship it, they won't always know what is valuable. While you may have your items insured, some things you just don't want to part with.

—*KALI COFFMAN*
LONDON, ENGLAND

• • • • • • • •

MAKE SURE EVERYTHING IS READY to go before your friends come over to help you, because there's nothing worse for them than having to sit and wait while you pack.

—*ANONYMOUS*
CASTLE ROCK, COLORADO
5 MOVES

• • • • • • • •

Request to have antique furniture custom crated.

—*DENVER AQUINO*
LAS VEGAS,
NEVADA
7 MOVES

MY HUSBAND'S COMPANY PAID FOR US to move from Colorado to Kansas. The movers came to our house, packed up everything, labeled and made very detailed, color-coded checklists of what was in each box to keep us organized. Then, they put the boxes on the truck and met us out there a few days later, unloaded everything and put it in the correct rooms. This would've cost about $12,000 if we'd paid out-of-pocket.

—*CANDICE PORTER*
OVERLAND PARK, KANSAS
5 MOVES

• • • • • • • •

CRAIGSLIST.COM IS THE BEST PLACE to advertise (for free!) and hire poor but strong college guys willing to earn some extra cash by moving your furniture for a couple of hours.

—*MELISSA CHAN*
NEW YORK, NEW YORK
4 MOVES

I HIRED PROFESSIONAL MOVERS for my last move just under a year ago. I noticed that rather than using bubble wrap, they used sheets of packing paper to line all of the boxes and then fill in the gaps. I was swimming in it every time a box was unpacked, but nothing was broken. I also kept my ultimate valuables in a separate small box, which came with me in the car and not the moving van. And I had a small suitcase, just in case something went wrong.

—LIZ SCHERER
    ANNAPOLIS, MARYLAND
     3 MOVES

Try to be gracious to the people who are helping you, even if one of their children scarfed down what was supposed to be a light lunch for 10.

—TODD MARTIN
    CONYERS, GEORGIA
    7 MOVES

IF YOU'RE HAVING FRIENDS OR FAMILY HELP with your move, be sure you have finished packing by the time they arrive to help schlep the boxes or load the truck. You should be completely ready to start moving by the time they walk through the door.

—MARY
    IOWA CITY, IOWA
    5 MOVES

TAKE ANYTHING THAT'S REALLY PRECIOUS—like jewelry and art—and move it yourself. For bigger things that you must trust to movers, take photos of them to prove that you had them and what condition they were in. Digital photos are great for that because they're free and once your things have arrived safely, you can just delete them.

—*SHANNON L.*
SAN RAFAEL, CALIFORNIA
4 MOVES

• • • • • • • • •

I USED THE INTERNET FOR MY LAST MOVE and regretted it. I found one of those movers who rent you part of a big semi. They estimate the cost, you load it, then they transport it to your destination. They ripped me off big time, saying my stuff weighed more than the average one bedroom apartment. I had to pay a wad of dough to get them to release my stuff at my new house. Also, this was a big semi with no ramp and no forklift. We had to lift really heavy stuff up and down several feet. Try loading a couch with a queen-size fold out bed in it up five feet. It ain't fun.

—*J.A.*
DURHAM, NORTH CAROLINA
16 MOVES

• • • • • • • • •

MOVES USUALLY DON'T GO SMOOTHLY. Anticipate problems and be understanding. If things go bad, pull everyone together and come up with a plan. Work together. It's easy to get frustrated. If your friend looks stressed, just say, "It's OK. I planned to come help. I understand that things didn't go as planned."

—*S.S.*
VIRGINIA BEACH, VIRGINIA
4 MOVES

MY FRIENDS AGREED TO HELP ME MOVE, but we never discussed specific dates. When I was finally ready, it turned out they couldn't help me because they were busy with work and school. I couldn't even use their truck, which I'd been counting on. So, by myself, I moved the entire contents of my house to my new place, which was 50 miles away. It took me a full 24-hour period and I had to make at least 10 trips. I spent a ton of money on gas and struggled to cram things like a couch, a dining room table and a bed into my '83 Cutlass. That's what you get for not thinking every last detail through.

—*LENNARD HAYNES SR.*
HOUSTON, TEXAS
6 MOVES

• • • • • • • •

WE USED ONE OF THE MOST RESPECTED movers in Calgary. They came with a team of four guys and moved the entire house in about eight hours or so. They were very professional and fast. I recommend a mover to anyone with a house. It saves a ton of hard work, and the cost is reasonable when you factor in how much easier it makes your move.

—*BART G. FARKAS*
COCHRANE, ALBERTA, CANADA
8 MOVES

• • • • • • • •

BRING ONLY WHAT YOU NEED and keep Coronas on hand. When I moved in Tucson with my dad and a friend we called it a "four-Corona move." Later when we fixed a deck we called it a "ten-Corona day"; it made it fun.

—*COURTNEY CRAIG*
SAN DIEGO, CALIFORNIA
6 MOVES

To the moon! The annual mileage of North American U-Haul trucks would move a family to the moon and back more than seven times per day, every day of the year.

—*U-HAUL*

IF YOU'RE SHIPPING YOUR CAR, don't try to pack a lot of belongings in it and get them to your new home that way. The shipping companies don't allow that for liability reasons.

—*LAURA VINCENT*
NOVATO, CALIFORNIA
2 MOVES

YOU LOVE YOUR BROTHER, BUT . . .

Never ask your 18-year-old brother and his exceptionally intelligent friends to help you move. My brother has a big truck and I thought, what better way to save money? So he and his friend went to pick up my couch and dining room table from my grandparents' house, where it had been in storage. They showed up at my new apartment that afternoon, minus my dining room table and two of the four cushions.

The best and worst part of the story is they weren't really sure where they lost everything along the 30-minute trip between my grandparents' house and mine. They just put everything in the bed of the truck, but didn't tie it down—or even put the tailgate up! I can laugh about this story now, but only because I am no longer sitting on the wooden boards of a couch with no cushions.

—*L.N.*
PHOENIX, ARIZONA
6 MOVES

A NUMBER OF STORAGE COMPANIES these days offer giant crates—"pods," they call them—to move your stuff inexpensively from one place to the next. When my father died, my sister and I used these crates to move all his stuff from Northern California to Atlanta. They dropped off the crates in the driveway, we loaded them up, they picked them up and took them to a warehouse and shipped them across the country for us. Some companies also offer to pack and unpack your crates for you. Best of all, the price is reasonable. We would have spent more on a U-Haul truck, and that would have entailed us doing all the work.

—JWAIII
ATLANTA, GEORGIA
15 MOVES

• • • • • • • •

WE HAD A MOVING COMPANY that said they'd come and pack up everything and move it. They *literally* took our garbage, wrapped it, and moved it to our new house. The next time, I learned to prepare a little more, even for full-service movers.

—ANNE B.
SAN FRANCISCO, CALIFORNIA
3 MOVES

• • • • • • • •

I PULL A SURPRISE ATTACK WHEN ASKING my friends to help me move. I invite them to come over to hang out and when they're there I start packing and make them feel bad for just sitting on the couch and not helping. Basically, after they're already at my apartment, I pressure them into helping me. Be strategic about it and call up the friends that have the pickup truck and can help you lift boxes.

—G.P.
IOWA CITY, IOWA
5 MOVES

Hire some cute movers so when you are looking at "crack" all day it's actually enjoyable.

—ANONYMOUS
WALNUT CREEK, CALIFORNIA
5 MOVES

I DIDN'T KNOW THIS UNTIL I STARTED ASKING questions, but U-Haul bases its prices on the number of available vehicles in a specific location. So, theoretically, if you rent a U-Haul in California and drive it to Colorado, it might cost you $100 to drop it off in Denver, but only $30 to drop it off in Colorado Springs. Definitely spend some time calling around to check out your different options. The savings is definitely worth it!

—*J.C.*
REDMOND, WASHINGTON
15 MOVES

· · · · · · · ·

"**Don't ask anyone to help you move if you wouldn't want to go out to have a beer with them afterwards. You can't use them *just* to move.**"

—*DOMINIC STABILE*
FOREST HILL, MARYLAND
15-20 MOVES

· · · · · · · ·

MAKE SURE YOU HAVE SOME STRONG BOYS to help. My mom helped me move one time when my brother wasn't home and my dad was in the hospital. She has really bad knees, so I ended up having to lift most of the heavy stuff. What should have taken an hour took 5 hours. We'd carry something a few feet, then have to rest—and a few more feet, then rest—over and over again.

—*MINDY YOUNG*
DALLAS, TEXAS
6 MOVES

YOU SHOULD BE SO LUCKY . . .

When my dreaded moving day arrived, I couldn't believe I had managed to scrape together eight pick-up trucks, five dollies and twenty willing friends to help me move my huge two-bedroom apartment into my shiny-new three-bedroom house. With so much help, my apartment was packed up and tied down in under an hour. We drove to my new house where my wonderful workers stacked the labeled boxes into the appropriate rooms. While waiting for the promised pizza to be delivered, friends decided to unpack a few boxes.

Before the pizza arrived, my books had been dusted off and lovingly placed on the bookshelves. My kitchen had been unpacked and set up. My clothes were hanging in the appropriate closets. My bed was set up and made. My office was unpacked with my computer set up. My plants had been placed on their stands around the house based on their lighting requirements. My artwork had been hung and the knick-knacks were in their places.

When the sellers stopped by three hours after the start of my move, they caught a raging party in my backyard where we were eating pizza, barbecuing hot dogs and hamburgers and playing the first of many volleyball games. Oh, and the house was completely set up. I was home.

—HOLLY WINTER
DENVER, COLORADO

ALWAYS ASK TO BE THE FIRST MOVE OF THE DAY, otherwise your movers will arrive a few hours late.

> —*J.W.*
> *NEW YORK, NEW YORK*
> 🚚 *5 MOVES*

• • • • • • • •

ONE DAY, I SPOTTED A MOVING TRUCK on the street. Two guys had started a moving company called "Two Little Men with Big Hearts." That's exactly what they were—two short and strong guys with one truck. I ended up hiring them for one of my family's moves. It was fun, because they made me feel like I was moving with friends instead of strangers. The personalized attention that smaller companies can give made moving feel like much less of a chore.

> —*EMMILLIO E.*
> *VANCOUVER, BRITISH COLUMBIA, CANADA*
> 🚚 *7 MOVES*

We'll E-mail! Saying Goodbye to Friends and Family

If all that packing and organizing and decision-making (not to mention the thought of all the heavy lifting to come) isn't enough to keep you from moving, having to say goodbye to friends and family (or pets!) might be the straw that breaks the mover's back. But moving is also about saying goodbye, right? You're heading for a new adventure, a new life, buoyed by the experiences of the life you're leaving behind. So, chin up. Read on to learn how to leave your old life on the best possible terms.

BECAUSE YOU ONLY SAY GOODBYE to people you care about, try to make it a humorous event. Tears only make the trip to your new home longer. True friends will never leave you and will always only be a phone call away.

—TRAVONNIE N.
FRANKLIN, TENNESSEE
6 MOVES

GET EVERYBODY'S CONTACT INFORMATION.

—CHI-CHI
SILVER SPRING, MARYLAND
12 MOVES

I WROTE A LITTLE NOTE to each of my good friends when I was leaving town, telling them how much their friendship had meant to me and reminiscing over some fun memories. It was a bit of work, but it meant so much more than just sending out mass Christmas cards. I think it really inspired some of my friends to be better about keeping in touch and visiting.

—*K.T.*
BURLINGTON, VERMONT
5 MOVES

- - - - - - - -

SAYING GOODBYE IS ALWAYS HARDER than you think, especially if you drag it out. We haven't sold our old apartment yet and we still have enough furniture there to spend the night. We keep going back to the old neighborhood, getting nostalgic. We go to our favorite restaurants with friends who ask us, "Did you move yet?"

—*J.P.*
HOBOKEN, NEW JERSEY
8 MOVES

- - - - - - - -

IN THE ARMY, you have duty-free status, which means there's no tax on liquor. Plus, you can't ship booze home with you. So, when I was transferred back to the U.S. from Egypt, I had two choices: Pass my old alcohol down to a new arrival, or have an excellent going away party. I chose the latter, and some people got together with the remnants of my tequila, rum and vodka —one lady even made 100 Jell-O shots with each type of alcohol! The attitude is, if you bought it, you might as well have a good time with it. Plus, you can contribute to your own going away party, so others don't have to foot the entire bill.

—*DOUG BRIMMER*
COLORADO SPRINGS, COLORADO
10 MOVES

I PUT TOGETHER A SLIDE SHOW of our time in Boston before we left—it's pretty easy with digital photos—and had it running in the background of our goodbye party. Pretty soon, we were all gathered around watching and laughing over all the great memories.

—*SEAN H.*
NEW YORK, NEW YORK
12 MOVES

• • • • • • • •

KNOW THAT FOR EVERY FRIEND YOU HAVE to leave behind, you will make two new friends if you allow yourself to be open. I left over thirty years'-worth of friends when I came down to San Antonio but I decided that I was going to open myself up to what people can give. Even while we were looking for houses, I made nice friends; it was like they were trying to make a gift of San Antonio to us.

—*APRIL ROBINS ELLISON*
SAN ANTONIO, TEXAS
8 MOVES

WE'VE MOVED

Create "We've Moved" postcards on your computer with your new address, home phone, and cell number and send it out a few days before you move so your friends and family will get used to it and you won't lose any mail. Enjoy your new home!

—*SHONDA J. WAXMAN*
SAN JOSE, CALIFORNIA
4 MOVES

DON'T HAVE ONE MASSIVE GOODBYE PARTY, because you end up only talking to people for a couple minutes each and then you have to run off to the next person. Instead, get smaller groups of related friends/family for a series of goodbye activities—parties, meals, picnics, day-trips, whatever. That way you really can connect with the people you're leaving.

—*S. COLEMAN*
NEW YORK, NEW YORK
4 MOVES

. . . .

" When you move away, your friends stay with you and enemies disappear. "

—*JAMES NEWHOUSE*
CIBOLO, TEXAS
8 MOVES

. . . .

DON'T TAKE YOUR RELATIONSHIPS FOR GRANTED. You may intend to stay in one place forever, but you never know when you'll have to pack up and leave. I had lived in North Carolina all my life and had no intention of moving. Then I met my husband, who got a good job in Texas. Suddenly, after 28 years, I found myself saying goodbye to the family and friends I had grown up with. If being separated from them has taught me one thing, it's the importance of making the most of every moment you have together.

—*VANESSA HAIRSTON*
HIGHLANDS RANCH, COLORADO
2 MOVES

BECAUSE I FIND THIS PROCESS EMOTIONAL, I don't drag it out . . . I pretend it's not happening until the last minute. I act as though I'll see my friends for a long time to come. I don't give myself time to get sentimental and I've usually stopped to think about it only when I'm already on a plane, thinking about my next place.

—PHIL PROVART
TORONTO, ONTARIO, CANADA
 4 MOVES

• • • • • • • •

WHEN I MADE THE DECISION TO MOVE, the hardest part was telling my friends. They were upset, but in the months prior to my moving, we spent as much time as possible together. I don't think there's ever an easy way to tell someone you're leaving, but if you're upfront and honest about it, it's a lot easier to deal with.

—A.D.
HARRINGTON, MAINE
2 MOVES

• • • • • • • •

I HAD A GREAT PARTY AT MY HOUSE when I was moving. It was a popsicle party. It was August. I told them: We are moving, and we want to see you all again, and you don't have to prepare anything—just come over. It was really easy, entertaining and cheap.

—DEONA HOUFF
MOUNT SIDNEY, VIRGINIA
4 MOVES

• • • • • • • •

IT'S IMPORTANT TO STAY CLOSE, through phone calls and e-mails, with the people who you were close with in your old cities. It doesn't have to be goodbye for good, but "see you soon."

—JENNIFER DAVIS
LOS ANGELES, CALIFORNIA
7 MOVES

SOME PEOPLE HAVE A REAL HARD TIME saying goodbye. But it's really an important part of the moving on process. I think if you leave without saying your proper goodbyes it makes it harder to feel at home in your new place. Saying goodbye gives you closure and it enables you to "move on."

—*C.M.*
PITTSBURGH, PENNSYLVANIA
5 MOVES

. . . .

PERHAPS A COUPLE OF FRIENDS OR FAMILY members from your old place can come to your new place during your move to help ease the shock and work load involved with uprooting and relocating. You will still have to say goodbye, but they might feel better seeing you safe and secure in your new place. Plus, you can have memories of doing this together. It is also motivation for them to return and see you, to check your progress and see how you're managing.

—*JILL MARIE DAVIS*
WEEHAWKEN, NEW JERSEY
12 MOVES

THE LAST WORD: PARTY

The best way to say goodbye to an apartment (and to a landlord, if they were particularly nasty) is to throw a damn good party. The lousy part of renting is that you're at the mercy of someone else who owns the place, but the upshot of that is you don't give a damn when you're on the way out. Of course, the party will only be good if you have a "security deposit be damned" attitude.

—*TED*
TORONTO, ONTARIO, CANADA
5 MOVES

CARRY ON TRADITIONS YOU PRACTICED where you previously lived. It'll make the transition to a new place easier. Every January 1st, my friends and I in Milwaukee dove into the frozen water. It was the Polar Bear Club. When I moved to Syracuse, I continued that January 1st tradition here. It helped me feel connected to them despite the distance.

> —DAVID
> SYRACUSE, NEW YORK
> 6 MOVES

" Instead of a party in your house (which is in chaos because of the move), have your friends meet you for a fun potluck picnic/barbecue in the park. It's easier on the cleanup and a great way to spend lots of time hanging out with old friends. "

> —SAM
> SANTA MONICA, CALIFORNIA
> 13 MOVES

ALL I CAN SAY IS, THANK GOD FOR E-MAIL. It's so much easier to say goodbye to friends you are sad to leave when you know a conversation is always just a click away.

> —EMMA
> CHICAGO, ILLINOIS
> 6 MOVES

I miss my dog! We had to leave him behind. For our next move, we have to negotiate a contract that includes bringing our pets.

—*E.G.*
NEW HAVEN,
CONNECTICUT
3 MOVES

I MOVED FIVE TIMES IN THREE YEARS. The first time I was in a hurry and I didn't take time to say goodbye to everyone. But from that I learned the importance of taking the time—not on moving day, but a month or two before the move—to spend time with people I care about and tell them I love them and will miss them. It's so important to do that well in advance of the move.

—*LAURIE*
SAN DIEGO, CALIFORNIA

• • • • • • • •

THE BEST FRIENDS ARE THE KIND you don't have to say goodbye to. You may not talk to them for months, but when you see them or talk to them again, you can just pick up from where you left off.

—*B.H.*
VERNON HILLS, ILLINOIS
3 MOVES

• • • • • • • •

I NEVER USE THE WORD "GOODBYE." Goodbyes are much too hard and personal. Instead, I say stuff like, "I love you" or "Only five weeks until we see each other again." This reinforces the fact I will definitely be back, and makes leaving that much easier.

—*P.O.*
NEW BRUNSWICK, NEW JERSEY
6 MOVES

• • • • • • • •

OUR MOVE TO DENVER was incredibly positive. I recommend that everybody make a CD of their favorite "motivational songs" to play, as a symbol of leaving behind the old and moving toward the new. For us, the Dixie Chicks always inspire. And "Ain't No Mountain High Enough" sailed us all the way to the Rockies!

—*JANE DEBATTY*
DENVER, COLORADO
4 MOVES

WHEN MY PARENTS MOVED from my childhood home, it helped me to take photos of each room before and after. My family also spent time talking about memories and reminiscing about all the years we had there. It's very bittersweet to move—you know in your heart that change is a good thing and that new doors open when old ones close—but it's still hard to let go.

—STACY SILVER
TORONTO, ONTARIO, CANADA

• • • • • • • •

BEFORE YOU LEAVE A PLACE, go do all those famous tourist things you never did because you "had all the time in the world." If you're from New York City, everybody will ask you about the Statue of Liberty, the Empire State Building, Ground Zero, etc., and you'll want to have some sort of answer or description. Don't be so jaded that you miss out on those famous sites.

—JERRY B.
NEW YORK, NEW YORK
7 MOVES

• • • • • • • •

PHONE CALLS AND LETTERS WORK GREAT when you're trying to keep in touch with old friends, but you have to go beyond that. Every year, my friends and I pick a destination halfway between where we're living, and meet up for a girls only "spring break." This trip is a great bonding experience and tons of fun, but, most importantly, it reinforces the message that we're important to each other because we've made it a priority to take time off from work and buy a plane ticket. Your friends become your family as you get older. You have to treat them special and nurture those relationships.

—NIKKI KING
BEVERLY HILLS, CALIFORNIA
10 MOVES

THEY SAY THAT MOVING IS one of the most stressful things for your heart, and I think part of it is the tearful goodbyes.

—*MATT MARSHALL*
EVANS CITY, PENNSYLVANIA
🚚 *3 MOVES*

SHARING IS CARING

I left Texas in June, the same month as my birthday. My friends threw me a going away/birthday party. I really appreciated it. It was bittersweet. I walked into church, balloons were everywhere, and everybody yelled "Surprise!" They shared stories about me, saying some great things about me that made it a little more difficult to leave. I built great friendships for the two years I was in Corsicana. I felt encouraged but sad at the same time when I left the party because I knew I'd probably never see those people again. A week later, I was in New York.

But, I didn't leave anything behind. I told each and every one of them what they meant to me. I was specific about things we went through and just told them how much I enjoyed spending time with them and how much I was going to miss them. I didn't leave that party without everyone knowing how I felt. That's what I'd advise. You can't have any regrets. That made the move easier because I felt like I was sad, yeah, but my business was taken care of.

—*KEVIN BURNS*
SYRACUSE, NEW YORK

MOST PEOPLE HAVE A FAVORITE ROOM, view or place in their house—that's usually the hardest part to say goodbye to. For me, it was the backyard. I think it's important to take a long hard look and close your eyes. Whenever you're stressed, or miss "home," you can let your imagination take you back to that spot you love.

—ROCKY
TORONTO, ONTARIO, CANADA

• • • • • • • •

 Find a harmless place to leave your mark. When we moved in, we found the initials of the last family's kids in the post of the playground set. When we left, we had our kids scratch in their initials, too. **"**

—J.R.
CHICAGO, ILLINOIS
4 MOVES

• • • • • • • •

THE OLDER YOU GET THE MORE DIFFICULT it becomes to move. Yes, with age you develop a system, but it never gets easier. The emotional upheaval is always tough. When you're an adult the transition is tougher because you're completely responsible for everything—the actual move, the emotional upheaval—and you never truly know if the place you're headed will work out.

—JOHN W.
LONGMEADOW, MASSACHUSETTS

An estimated 42 million Americans move each year.

—US CENSUS BUREAU

BEST MOVING GIFTS

LITTLE THINGS LIKE DISH TOWELS AND PLATES AND CUPS either get lost in the shuffle or broken in the move. If you are going to buy someone a moving present I'd say keep it to something simple that they use every day and may be scrambling to find right after moving into the new place. We always use dish towels to pack glassware in the boxes so that the stuff doesn't break, but then when you need a towel you don't have one.

—*MIKE BELL*
CRANBERRY TOWNSHIP, PENNSYLVANIA
5 *MOVES*

· · · · · · · ·

IF YOU WANT TO BE HELPFUL, GIVE THEM CASH. My father picked up the cost of the moving truck for us once, and that was a big help. We were already strapped for cash because we had to come up with the security deposit and the first month's rent for our apartment.

—*TODD CHARLESWORTH*
BOSTON, MASSACHUSETTS
2 *MOVES*

· · · · · · · ·

WHEN WE MOVED INTO OUR FIRST HOME, my sister and her husband bought us this large decorative stone for the front yard that had our last name engraved in it. It was so cool. It made us feel like the place was really ours.

—*LEROY BROWN*
BRADDOCK, PENNSYLVANIA
2 *MOVES*

AFTER LIVING FOR TWO YEARS in Gramercy Park and the Lower East Side, I moved into my own apartment on the Upper East Side of Manhattan. As a housewarming gift, my friend went around my new neighborhood and collected all the takeout menus and put them in a binder for me. It was the most creative gift I had ever received.

—*J.M.*
NEW YORK, NEW YORK
? MOVES

. . . .

SOME OF THE BEST GIFTS MY WIFE AND I RECEIVED when we moved into our home were gift cards to home improvement centers, such as Home Depot and Lowe's. We had already made quite a few improvements to our home, but we had hundreds of dollars still to go! We were grateful for every cent!

—*MICHAEL REICH*
HELLERTOWN, PENNSYLVANIA
4 MOVES

Every place I go, I pick up a rock to remind me of everywhere I have been. It's one stepping stone at a time.

—*ENID NIEVES-CRUZ*
FT. HAMIL,
KENTUCKY
🚐 *3 OR 4 MOVES*

IT SOUNDS CLICHÉ, but if you are moving and leaving a lot of good friends, throw a party a week or so before you leave. If your place is in too much disarray, go out. Everyone will be in a good mood, so you'll remember them happy and cheerful, not complaining about their jobs and husbands.

> —*J. DANIELSON*
> *EVANSTON, ILLINOIS*
> 🚐 *3 MOVES*

• • • • • • • •

"WHEREVER YOU GO, THERE YOU ARE." In other words, home is wherever your stuff is. This country is basically the same from one end to the other, so don't get all worried about a move. They have McDonald's in your new town, too.

> —*SANDY J.*
> *ZELIENOPLE, PENNSYLVANIA*
> 🚚 *8 MOVES*

• • • • • • • •

TEN HAPPY MONTHS AGO WE MOVED OUT of the house we lived in for 35 years. I tell you, there's something wrong with the both of us. My husband and I never looked back. We're happy here. It wasn't sad to say goodbye to the house. My husband said for years he'd never move, but once he saw what we could get for our house, he said "Come on! Let's move!" Maybe we're senile—but we have each other.

> —*LAURETTA SORRENTINO*
> *LAKEWOOD, NEW JERSEY*
> 🚐 *4 MOVES*

It's Moving Day! Going from Here to There

Are you ready? Your answer doesn't really matter, of course, because—ready or not—moving day has arrived. It's time to lift (with your legs!) and direct and trip over things and lose your patience and wonder if all your stuff will be broken (or lost) when you get to where you're going. If you're doing it yourself, you even get to drive a gigantic truck through traffic! Fret not. We're here to help you transport the goods as safely and efficiently as possible. So, are you ready?

IF I COULD ONLY TAKE ONE THING with me it would be my sense of humor. That way I could get through having to replace all my worldly possessions without going crazy. And it wouldn't take up too much space.

—SANDRA FONKOUA
SILVER SPRING, MARYLAND
1 MOVE

BRING A SAW FOR ANY WOOD THAT NEEDS TO COME OFF.

—REBECCA HUENINK
WAUWATOSA,
WISCONSIN
5 MOVES

HAVE SNACKS FOR YOUR MOVERS and helpers. Food is an icebreaker and it is thoughtful. Have plastic cups, paper towels, bath tissue and bottled water handy for the same reasons.

> —JILL
> WEEHAWKEN, NEW JERSEY
> 12 MOVES

Pack an overnight bag. You won't remember what box you tossed your razor into.

—APRIL SMITH
BOSTON,
MASSACHUSETTS

• • • • • • • •

BE CAREFUL NOT TO STRAIN YOURSELF. I've thrown my back out so many times and usually when this happens, you don't even feel it right away. Instead, you wake up really sore a couple of days later.

> —LUCIA BOLES
> ST. LOUIS, MISSOURI
> 6 MOVES

• • • • • • • •

MAKE SURE NO BONEHEADED FRIENDS TAPE the drawers or lids of good furniture shut. It totally messes up the finish.

> —SARA CLEMENCE
> ALBANY, NEW YORK
> 12 MOVES

• • • • • • • •

FIND A PACE THAT'S COMFORTABLE and always lift with your knees. I fell down a flight of stairs helping a friend move because we were rushing. We were lifting a mattress. The stairway was narrow and twisted a lot. The mattress hit me in the face and I fell back. Later, we were trying to lift a dresser that had to weigh 600 pounds. No lie. I tried to pull with my back. I had to go to the hospital. I was there for two and a half hours. I strained muscles on both sides of my spine.

> —DOMINIQUE COLEMAN
> SYRACUSE, NEW YORK
> 5 MOVES

IF YOU'RE MOVING YOURSELF, make sure everything is tied down. I mistakenly thought a rocking chair was secure by itself in the back of my El Camino, even though my wife tried to warn me otherwise. Well, just as I was building up speed on the freeway, guess what flew out? A few inches of rope can prevent 30 years of unpleasant reminders.

—*JOE HOLLIMAN*
CENTENNIAL, COLORADO
2 MOVES

. . . .

❝ What you need for moving is lots of boxes, and big bottles of bourbon and Tylenol. It is so painful and overwhelming that you need to be a little bit out of it to do it well. ❞

—*LINDA REEVES*
SAN ANTONIO, TEXAS
15 MOVES

. . . .

THERE ARE CERTAIN CONSTANTS that one should always prepare for when moving. #1: You always have more stuff than you remember. #2: Your car/truck is always smaller than it looks, especially when you start packing stuff in it. #3: You will always, inadvertently, throw something away that you really, really need. #4: Even if you make a concerted effort to lift with your legs, your back will always hurt the next day.

—*BRONLEA HAWKINS*
BELLINGHAM, WASHINGTON
3 MOVES

HELLO, DOLLY!

IF YOUR RENTAL TRUCK COMPANY OFFERS THE USE OF A DOLLY, take it! When I moved, my husband was deployed and I had to move everything to our apartment with just my sister's help. I didn't know how I was going to manage all the heavy furniture. With the dolly, we were able to move everything—from boxes to sofas—all in one day!

> —*ALLISON BENOIT*
> *HOUMA, LOUISIANA*
> 🚚 *3 MOVES*

* * * * * * * * *

IF YOU'RE A GUY, YOU SHOULD SUCK UP your pride and hire a dolly. It'll save your back and be the best ten bucks you ever spent.

> —*B.N.*
> *MINNEAPOLIS, MINNESOTA*
> 🚚 *4 MOVES*

* * * * * * * *

MAKE SURE THAT YOU HAVE PLENTY of trash bags. I personally have only moved once in my adult life but I have helped many other people move, and there are never enough trash bags.

> —*C.S.A.*
> *BELLINGHAM, MASSACHUSETTS*
> 🚚 *1 TIME*

INVOLVE AS MANY PEOPLE AS YOU CAN possibly stand. Pay as much money as you can afford to have it done by professionals. When we moved, all of our uncles brought their farm trucks and loaded the big stuff in them. The aunts stayed at the house and were ready to unload kitchen stuff as soon as it got there. When everything was in the house, they prepared food for everyone, ate with us, and cleaned up the kitchen they had organized for me.

> —*JANE FLEMING ROSENBOHM*
> *HANNA CITY, ILLINOIS*
> *12 MOVES*

Mattresses and mirrors should be placed along the walls of the truck and tied securely.

> —*HOMEDEPOT*
> *MOVING.COM*

Don't sweat it. Seriously. The moment you start to break a sweat, stop working. It's not worth it.

> —*JUSTIN P.*
> *NEW YORK, NEW YORK*

DON'T ASSUME THAT JUST BECAUSE you're moving across town you can rent a truck for "just the big stuff" and haul "the small stuff" over a little at a time. I thought, "The big stuff is all that matters." Wrong. You have so much small stuff that it probably equals twice the big stuff in weight and space.

> —*JWAIII*
> *ATLANTA, GEORGIA*
> *15 MOVES*

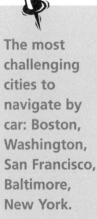

The most challenging cities to navigate by car: Boston, Washington, San Francisco, Baltimore, New York.

—*Sperling's Best Places*

KEEP EVERYBODY MOVING. Even if they're carrying small boxes, they're moving the rock. If you give people an excuse to stand around, they will.

—*Evan*
Atlanta, Georgia
15 moves

• • • • • • • •

LAUGH IT OFF. Things will go wrong. Things will break. On our move to Florida the boat's cover flew off on the highway. We caught it in time, pulled over, and laughed.

—*D.D.*
Palm Beach Gardens, Florida
5 moves

• • • • • • • •

DO NOT LEAVE YOUR HAZARD LIGHTS in your U-Haul blinking as you move. When you try to start the engine and hear a clicking sound, it means that your battery has died. Trust me—you don't want to deal with this.

—*Amy Hirotaka*
Brooklyn, New York
4 moves

• • • • • • • •

MAKE SURE YOU READ—and follow—the instructions on vehicle speed if you're doing any towing. I was towing a full-size Cadillac from Denver to Phoenix, and the warning on the tow package said DO NOT EXCEED 55 MPH. So there I was doing 80, and the vehicle started swaying back and forth in an uncontrolled manner. Those warnings are there for a reason!

—*J.C.*
Redmond, Washington
15 moves

GIVE MOVING VAN DRIVERS A MAP! My three sons and I awaited a moving van from North Carolina at our new home in Roanoke, Virginia. The van was due at our place in the morning. By lunch time we were wondering, and just before 2 p.m. I called the agent. Seems the guys had taken off for a Virginia city that also began with "R"—Richmond, to be precise. That was across the state from us, and they arrived about dinnertime. As tired as they were, they unloaded until 2 a.m. and the job was finished. I offered them the pullout couch in the basement, but they thanked me and left—in the right direction I hope.

> —*BARBARA BRYAN*
> *DAVIDSON, NORTH CAROLINA*
> *2 MOVES*

* * * * * * * *

MY REFRIGERATOR FIT PERFECTLY in my old house. To get it into my new home, however, I had to take its doors off so the handles wouldn't get in the way. It only took me ten minutes because I was carrying the tools with me. If I wasn't, however, that would've been a pain.

> —*LENNARD HAYNES SR.*
> *HOUSTON, TEXAS*
> *6 MOVES*

* * * * * * * *

TAKE CAREFUL STOCK OF THE EQUIPMENT you're renting. My boyfriend was driving our U-Haul and I happened to look out the side-view mirror and see a door flapping behind us on the highway. We came close to having the contents of our lives spill out on the roadway. Turns out the U-Haul had a defective latching mechanism on the back door.

> —*ALYSSA AGEE*
> *SNOQUALMIE, WASHINGTON*
> *10 MOVES*

The most important thing to remember is that no matter how you get the stuff in there the truck has to be as full as possible before you leave. The tighter it's packed the less likely stuff will shift around and break.

—*JIM R.*
PITTSBURGH,
PENNSYLVANIA
6 MOVES

WHEN DRIVING A BIG VAN, only go forward if possible. Go straight back if absolutely necessary. But never, ever try to do anything as complicated as a five point turn!

—CHRISTINE B.
NEW YORK, NEW YORK
6 MOVES

❝❝Moving vans aren't designed for petite women. Make sure you have a driving cushion so you can see over the steering wheel.❞❞

—STEPH D.
BALTIMORE, MARYLAND
4 MOVES

MAKE SURE YOU DRIVE ON WIDE ROADS. I once drove a moving truck down a pretty narrow road, with trees hanging near the edge. Sure enough, the side rearview nailed a branch and shattered. Also, if you must back up, particularly while at the gas station, have someone jump out and see if anything's behind you. I failed to do this and I backed into a tiny sports car, which had pulled up so close I couldn't see it in the (shattered) rearview.

—JWAIII
ATLANTA, GEORGIA
15 MOVES

AS YOU PACK THE TRUCK, try to put boxes from the same room together, e.g. put all the kitchen boxes in the same place in the truck. Pack your boxes for your bedroom last, so you can put your bed together, complete with sheets and blankets, first. That way, when you've had enough, you can go to sleep.

—*L.A.*
IOWA CITY, IOWA
4 MOVES

• • • • • • • •

DRIVING THE MOVING TRUCK ISN'T AS HARD as it looks. You'll get the hang of it quicker than you think. What I learned is to 'live' in the mirrors. The mirrors on a big truck are much more important than on your passenger car. You really have to pay attention to what is happening on all sides of you at all times. And if you are not sure if you can make it, don't try.

—*BEN NOBLE*
YOUNGSTOWN, PENNSYLVANIA
3 MOVES

WHEN THE LIVIN' WAS EASY

Easiest move for me? My first move with my husband. We were young and had nothing. We just kept saying to ourselves, "Nothing to move and nothing to lose!" It almost became our mantra. Everything fit into his Camaro. That was so easy and pretty cool, too! Still, we drove that Camaro from Florida to Rhode Island in the winter. Imagine bringing only sandals to Rhode Island in December—during a blizzard! We quickly started buying lots of clothes. We were more prepared for our second move.

—*SUE*
DESTIN, FLORIDA
9 MOVES

LOOK, MA! NO HANDS!

MATTRESSES ARE NOT MEANT TO BE CARRIED ON THE ROOF of your car. It looks silly, it's an aerodynamic faux pas, and it's downright dangerous. My friend Eric and I discovered this when I helped him move many years ago. He didn't have much stuff, and it was a short move, so we figured why waste the $50 on renting a truck? We packed the car with all his stuff, then slapped the mattress on the roof with one little rope for luck, and drove off.

We forgot to consider that when a car is in motion, it must move a lot of air out of the way, and most of this air moves straight up, right underneath the mattress. We got about halfway there before the first string broke. Naturally we didn't have any extra string with us, so we did the obvious: We each rolled down our windows and grabbed onto the mattress handles. What a ride! Anything over about 15 mph and we were being lifted out of our seats. It was like riding a hang glider. Not to mention that it's hard enough to drive with only one hand without the added challenge of being pulled out of the car.

We made it safely, mostly due to luck, not common sense. Next time, however, I'm paying for the truck.

—*KEVIN SHOLANDER*
FORT COLLINS, COLORADO
9 *MOVES*

LEARN TO USE YOUR MIRRORS. In a car, you can strain around and look to see what's behind and beside you. In a truck, you can't do this. You have to adjust your mirrors appropriately before you start, and trust them. Then make sure you signal and move slowly.

—*EVAN*
ATLANTA, GEORGIA
15 MOVES

* * * * * * * *

THERE IS NO SUCH THING as "seating for three" in a U-Haul. This purported "third seat" was nothing more than the hump over the transmission, wedged in between two regular seats. A thousand miles and three aching butts later (from taking turns on that seat), we were ready to throw that truck into the Hudson River.

—*RICHARD G. CALO*
EAGLE BRIDGE, NEW YORK
15 MOVES

* * * * * * * *

TO KEEP THE TRUCK IN ITS LANE, you have to make sure the middle of the hood is even with the curb—and if you're on the passenger side, the middle of the hood should be even with the yellow line on the street.

—*PAULA CANNELLA*
EATONTOWN, NEW JERSEY
5 MOVES

Before you try to move, you have to learn to say, "Oh well!" when things don't go right, and move on.

—*MARGARET*
BELLEVUE,
WASHINGTON
3 MOVES

LOAD THINGS INTO THE MOVING VAN in the order in which you want to organize things when you get to your destination. Pack everything securely and evenly distribute the weight. Most of all, plan ahead and take your time. There's nothing more stressful than waiting until the last minute.

—*J. M. CORNWELL*
TABERNASH, COLORADO
11 MOVES

• • • • • • • •

WHEN I MOVED, I started with the lightest stuff—pillows, bedding, etc., thinking that I would get all that stuff out of the way first. But it was a huge mistake. By the time the end of the day came, I was tired as a dog . . . and I still had the heaviest stuff left to carry!

—*NEILLY K.*
NEW YORK, NEW YORK
3 MOVES

• • • • • • • •

THE KEY IS TO HAVE EVERYTHING READY to be put in the truck all at the same time. You can't still be boxing stuff up while the truck is being loaded. Once everything is ready to go you can look at it and figure out in your mind how it would all fit best together inside the truck.

—*ROB JONES*
PITTSBURGH, PENNSYLVANIA
4 MOVES

• • • • • • • •

DON'T OPEN THE TRUCK if you think you hear something break along the way. It's a recipe for disaster trying to re-pack on the road, or deal with the heartbreak of the demise of granny's lamp on the highway. Just wait until you get where you're going.

—*PETER STEUR*
BRISBANE, AUSTRALIA
7 MOVES

LAMPSHADES ARE THE WORST. Movers pack them in light boxes without enough padding. Then they have a tendency to put them under boxes of books or exercise machines. Crunch. Their insurance pays by the pound. Oh, that lampshade? Here's seventy-five cents.

> —NAN ANDREWS AMISH
> EL GRANADA, CALIFORNIA
> 10 MOVES

. . . .

"I always start with the upstairs; it's like starting out going uphill at the beginning of a bike ride. When you're finished, it's literally all downhill from there."

> —ASHLEY KNOTTS
> ANDERSON, INDIANA
> 10 MOVES

. . . .

MY HUSBAND PLACES THE HEAVIEST ITEMS toward the back so the weight is centered. That way, while we're driving, we can avoid fishtailing or dragging the bottom if we hit a bump. That could be extremely destructive!

> —L.A.
> CLEVELAND, OHIO
> 11 MOVES

HEAVY LIFTING

One of the most trying, dangerous parts of moving is attempting to lift things like sofa beds and wooden armoires. Here are some helpful ideas for what to do when gravity is working against you.

I BROUGHT MY PARENTS' SOFA-BED with me to school. My father and teenage brother were struggling to get it through the tight doorway when the mother of the boy next door (an incredibly stout Irish woman who had clearly raised her share of rough boys) virtually threw the couch over her shoulder and hoisted it through the doorway. We all stood there dumbfounded as she set the couch down and walked away as if it were nothing.

—*J.H.*
CHICAGO, ILLINOIS
🚚 *4 MOVES*

· · · · · · · · ·

WHEN WE MOVED TO AMSTERDAM, the stairs in our new building were narrow and winding, so there was no way they could get the furniture up that way, especially the big sectional. Then, I noticed a lot of the old buildings have hooks that hang from the roof tops. That hook was used to hoist our furniture up and bring it in the front window, including the sectional.

—*TED CIOCHON*
ATLANTA, GEORGIA
🚚 *7 MOVES*

· · · · · · · · ·

MY HUSBAND RECENTLY HAD BACK SURGERY, so he can't lift heavy furniture. We had to move a 100+ pound safe into our basement, so we slid it onto a large, flat board that was about an inch thick and shimmied it down the stairs. It was perfect: Neither of us had to exert any energy and when we reached the bottom, we just slid the safe into place. Our floors didn't get scraped and we didn't get hurt. Who could ask for more?

—*P.O.*
NEW BRUNSWICK, NEW JERSEY
🚚 *6 MOVES*

I MEASURE THE DIMENSIONS of my moving truck ahead of time, then build a cardboard model-to-scale of the van space and my furniture. It only takes about an hour, and you can do it while you're watching TV. You can then arrange where everything is going to fit ahead of time without getting exhausted from a ton of heavy lifting. This saves a ton of time on moving day.

—*ASHLEY KNOTTS*
ANDERSON, INDIANA
10 MOVES

• • • • • • • •

PUT YOUR TV ON THE COUCH, and make sure its screen is facing toward the back. The padding will provide instant protection from vibration during the course of the move, and the screen is less likely to get scratched.

—*J.C.*
REDMOND, WASHINGTON
15 MOVES

• • • • • • • •

WHEN YOU'RE PACKING THE TRUCK, load the boxes first, then the big items—we learned that the hard way. The last time we moved, my brilliant husband said, "Let's get the couch and the table into the truck first." We were left with these big gaps we couldn't fill. You can't fit too much stuff on a table or a couch. The move ended up taking a lot longer because we had to re-organize about five different times.

—*CHRISTY LINDSKOG*
EL PASO, TEXAS
8 MOVES

• • • • • • • •

DON'T PANIC IF SOMETHING IS BROKEN in a move—there's always a chance it can be repaired.

—*ANONYMOUS*
READING, PENNSYLVANIA
4 MOVES

Put all boxes into one room so you don't have to run around the house like a madman on the big day.

—*ANONYMOUS*
CASTLE ROCK,
COLORADO
5 MOVES

DOUBLE CHECK THAT YOU WILL HAVE A PLACE to park your truck and unload the contents. Some buildings have strict rules about parking. If you can get a reserved parking sign for that day, do it. Some cities will let you reserve a couple of spots for moving trucks. It is safer than double parking and clogging up traffic.

—*J.M.D.*
WEEHAWKEN, NEW JERSEY
12 MOVES

. . . .

" Before the movers arrive, have as many of the boxes right by the door as possible. I try to put the stuff out on the curb. Then the movers just have to take the big stuff and go. "

—*SCOTT TOBIN*
LOS ANGELES, CALIFORNIA

. . . .

WATCH WHERE YOU THROW OUT THE TRASH! When I was moving to a new house I went through everything and piled up lots of clutter to throw away. I asked my son and his buddy to take this trash to the dump for me. Instead, they left it on a remote piece of land, without telling me. Six months later, I got a call from a woman saying that she found all of this trash on her property and the magazines had my name on them. I was horrified!

—*BARBARA STEVENS*
GATLINBURG, TENNESSEE
12 MOVES

GET A LANYARD THAT YOU CAN PUT around your neck and attach all necessary keys to it. DO NOT TAKE IT OFF while moving. I once sealed my front door key into a moving box. Another friend locked the U-Haul key . . . in the U-Haul.

—SARA CLEMENCE
ALBANY, NEW YORK
12 MOVES

• • • • • • • •

I LIKE TO LOAD DOWN ONE SIDE of the truck first, then the second side, so that it fills to the same height as the first. You want to step each successive row down. In other words, as you work toward the back you want each row of boxes to be a few inches lower than the top of the previous row so that the previous row won't move. It's like building a dam behind each row so that items can't shift in transit.

—M.E.W.
GLADSTONE, OREGON
10 MOVES

• • • • • • • •

USE THAT BIG SHELF up over the cab to load boxes only. Look at loading them in there like putting a puzzle together. Make it fit as tight as you can. Then put your couch and loveseat on opposite sides of the truck. Take the cushions off them and stack stuff on top of them. Between the two couches you should line up all your big appliances. Just put the fridge, stove, washer and dryer right down the middle of the truck between the two couches. That will keep all that big stuff in place. Fill in the gaps with the smaller stuff.

—TOBY WALTON
YOUNGSTOWN, OHIO
7 MOVES

✔

No matter how capable your movers or how good your packing skills are, you have to put your computer in the front seat of someone's car—do NOT pack it in the truck.

—STEVEN A. PARSONS JR.
FT. ASHBY, WEST VIRGINIA
2 MOVES

SECURE THE DRESSER DRAWERS using a long piece of string and tie it vertically around and knot. When your dresser is carried, the drawers won't fall out and the string is non-damaging to the paint (as tape would be). Just cut with scissors when ready to remove, and throw away.

—BETHANY AMBROSE
BALTIMORE, MARYLAND
4 MOVES

• • • • • • • •

THERE'S A REAL ART TO PACKING too much stuff into a space the size of a small bathroom with a four-foot ceiling. You have to start with the big stuff—couches, dressers, dining tables. The dressers always go along a wall, facing out, so if you've removed the drawers to make it lighter, you can put them back in. Leave the drawers full, too. No point wasting that space. Big tables are best turned upside down so more furniture or boxes can be stacked on top. Bookshelves should be upright if possible so you can stack boxes on them. Try and think in layers, back to front and bottom to top, each layer should be secure and able to bear weight. Just like Lego.

—FRED
WASHINGTON, DC
12 MOVES

• • • • • • • •

WHEN CARRYING LARGE PIECES OF FURNITURE, always grab first so you can make sure you are not walking backwards. That guy always gets the worst of it in a fall.

—J.W.
NEW YORK, NEW YORK
5 MOVES

THE ART OF PACKING A TRUCK

First of all, make sure you've got a lot of rope. And get a lot of the big stuff out there first, especially the heavy pieces. Find whatever pieces fit as flush against the front wall as possible, and start putting them in. The whole process is like fitting the pieces of a puzzle together.

Fill the front overhang with boxes, chests, etc. Make sure the heavy pieces, like sofas, go near the front. Turn tables upside down and lay them on sofas. Pack boxes, pillows, cushions, etc., around table legs. Set one chair in the truck right-side up, the other one upside down on top of it. Put small boxes, lampshades, children's toys, odds and ends under the bottom chair and on top of the top chair.

Stand mattresses and box springs on their sides at either side of the truck and slide headboards, paintings and mirrors between them. Push sofas, tables, boxes, etc. against the mattresses to keep them upright.

Stack things up to the roof, if you can, putting lighter stuff on top, but make sure that everything is stable and solid. Then, every five or six feet, rope that section off. Tie the rope to a hook on one side of the truck and run it across the exposed end of the stack, wrapping it around sofa legs, chairs, boxes, anything that will restrain the load. Tie the rope to a hook on the other side, and you're ready to start the next section.

—J.C.
ATLANTA, GEORGIA
9 MOVES

BATTLE OF THE BOXES

THE KEY TO MOVING IS WHOM YOU MARRY. Have a well-organized, structured wife who demands enormous things from the people she hires.

> —*GENE GREEN*
> *COLUMBIA, SOUTH CAROLINA*
> 🚚 *5 MOVES*

• • • • • • • •

BEAR IN MIND THAT YOU AND YOUR HUSBAND might have very different moving styles. I, for instance, feel compelled to unpack as many boxes as possible right away, while my husband prefers to unpack a little bit every day. Rather than fighting this, take advantage of it. Delegate accordingly.

> —*ANONYMOUS*
> *READING, PENNSYLVANIA*
> 🚐 *4 MOVES*

• • • • • • • •

NEVER, NEVER, NEVER LET YOUR HUSBAND PACK YOUR HOUSE when preparing for a move. The one time I let my husband do it, he didn't mark anything, and the boxes would have, like, one left shoe, a tire iron, a dirty fork, an unopened can of soda, an almost-empty box of fabric softener sheets and a souvenir sombrero. That was a frustrating couple of days.

> —*KRISTEN RAMSEY*
> *LOS ANGELES, CALIFORNIA*
> 🚚 *11 MOVES*

• • • • • • • •

IF YOU HAVE A HUSBAND LIKE MINE who has no decorating taste whatsoever, use the move as a time to put your mark on your new home. Tell him to stick to the physical move and let you handle the setting up. Buy new drapes, get new accessories for the bathroom. Experiment. But, most importantly, keep him out of the process.

> —*SHIRL MAWHINNEY*
> *PORTERSVILLE, PENNSYLVANIA*
> 🚐 *3 MOVES*

DO NOT MOVE DURING THE HOTTEST MONTH of the year. I moved in August in New York City, using a U-Haul and my scrawny roommate to move everything.

> —*AMY HIROTAKA*
> *BROOKLYN, NEW YORK*
> *4 MOVES*

. . . .

STAY CALM and remember that you are receiving much exercise from this endeavor.

> —*LIZ HERTNECK*
> *WASHINGTON, DC*
> *MOVED A BUNCH OF TIMES*

. . . .

BUNGEE CORDS. BUY AS MANY AS YOU THINK you will need and then buy some more. They are so valuable during a move. You can secure all your stuff in the truck by stringing those things all over the place. The bungee cord is a mover's most valuable tool. *(Ed. note: But be careful! Bungee cords can be dangerous! See, e.g., http://www.scif.com/news-info/lc-bulletins/ bungee.htm.)*

> —*JIM MORRISON*
> *PITTSBURGH, PENNSYLVANIA*
> *3 MOVES*

. . . .

WHEN TOWING YOUR CAR BEHIND A TRAILER, plan ahead before pulling into a parking lot. The first time we didn't and found ourselves in a dead-end. We had to take the car off the truck to back out.

> —*CLAUDE GRUENER*
> *AUSTIN, TEXAS*
> *15 MOVES*

MY BROTHER HAD A DRESSER that we could not get out of his second-floor bedroom. We couldn't imagine how he got it in there in the first place, and he didn't remember. We tried every angle possible but it just wouldn't go. We spent a good hour working on it until he remembered that it had actually been hoisted up through the window. So out the window it went.

—*MITZIE HAGEN*
  WHEELING, WEST VIRGINIA

Caution: Worst Moves Ever, Ahead

Not to be superstitious, but moving seems to bring out the bad luck in people. And, somewhere along the way to your new home, something will go wrong with your move. Knock on wood, it will probably be a minor incident. However, there are some unlucky folks who have encountered their own "worst move ever." Was it bad luck or bad planning? You be the judge. Be glad these stories aren't yours. (And just in case, better spit three times.)

WHETHER YOU'RE MOVING YOURSELF or paying professionals, the only thing you can plan on is something going wrong. In two moves, I've endured parking tickets, having the cops called on me, a truck breakdown in the middle of Pennsylvania, and a dropped TV.

> —SASHA EMMONS
> BROOKLYN, NEW YORK
> 7 MOVES

NEVER MOVE IN WITH YOUR MOTHER-IN-LAW.

—P.W.
CHICAGO, ILLINOIS
7 MOVES

WATCH THE WEATHER REPORT, and make sure the day you move is clear. We used open-bed pick-up trucks and halfway through our hour-and-a-half drive, there was a torrential downpour. When we finally got to our new place, which didn't have a garage, we had to spend two hours moving our stuff inside while getting drenched. At least thirty percent of our stuff was ruined.

—*JOHN COOKE*
GREELEY, COLORADO
 3 MOVES

. . . .

MOST DIFFICULT MOVE: to El Paso, Texas! I absolutely hated the city. I had not visited it before we moved there. I figured that I would settle in eventually, but I never did. It was a terrible experience. My advice: Check out the city before you officially move there. Stay for several weeks, if possible. It's a nightmare to discover that you hate a city just as the moving truck is driving up to deliver your furniture!

—*BETH*
OKLAHOMA
8 MOVES

. . . .

MAKE SURE THE TRAILER IS THE RIGHT SIZE for your car. I moved from Berkeley to New York and rented a trailer from U-Haul to hitch on the back of my car. One hour into the trip my car started to overheat. I had to keep pulling over and finally called a tow truck and got my car to a garage. The transmission gave out completely in Topeka, Kansas. When I finally arrived in New Jersey, the car was totally dead. The trip was only a week long, but I'm sure it took a month off my lifespan!

—*BILL BRAZELL*
BROOKLYN, NEW YORK
16 MOVES

THE HARDEST MOVE I EVER MADE was simply across town. Because I didn't have enough money to hire a moving company, I just had a few friends who helped. But I had to lift most of the heavy stuff like the sofa, dresser, and cabinets myself. That's how I hurt my back. I have been seeing a chiropractor and doctor for more than a decade now.

—*MILLETTE R.*
VALLEJO, CALIFORNIA
5 MOVES

• • • • • • • •

" Once I moved on a Saturday when it was 20 degrees below zero with the wind chill! It took 12 guys just 4 hours to move my houseful of belongings. It was so cold, everyone wanted to keep moving! "

—*ED REICH*
DUBOIS, PENNSYLVANIA
4 MOVES

• • • • • • • •

WE BOUGHT OUR HOME FROM A COUPLE going through a divorce. It was a moving nightmare. They had been out of the house for four months, but had left things in the cupboards and there was an unplugged freezer in the basement with rotting food in it. Of course, there were mice in there, too!

—*DELLA D.*
BRIDGEPORT, NEW YORK
7 MOVES

LOST & NOT FOUND

WE LOST A TOASTER IN OUR LAST MOVE. We still haven't found it. It's crazy. It was obviously sucked into the vortex of "the move."

> —BART G. FARKAS
> COCHRANE, ALBERTA, CANADA
> 8 MOVES

• • • • • • • •

DURING ONE MOVE, I lost a chair. It must have fallen out of the truck en route because I never did find it. When hauling things in the back of a pick-up truck, you have to drive slow and make sure everything is secure and accounted for.

> —JAMES PLAMBECK
> DAVENPORT, IOWA
> 3 MOVES

• • • • • • • •

YOU KNOW HOW PEOPLE JOKE that clothes dryers eat socks? I think moving vans do the same thing, but not with socks. It's usually something fairly small and insignificant that we don't realize is missing right away. But it never fails. One time I lost the mouse from my computer and never found it. Another time it was a box of fax paper. Maybe my friends are stealing my stuff?

> —JONATHAN BARNES
> CUMBERLAND, MARYLAND
> 2 MOVES

• • • • • • • •

I'VE NEARLY LOST MY MIND during a few moves. But nothing of value, no.

> —JOHN RODGERS
> SEATTLE, WASHINGTON
> 6 MOVES

DOES MY SANITY COUNT? Yes, of course I've lost items during moves. Luckily for me it hasn't been anything particularly important or irreplaceable.

—*TODD MARTIN*
CONYERS, GEORGIA
🚚 *7 MOVES*

• • • • • • • • •

OUR MOVER PUT ALL OF THE HARDWARE from our disassembled furniture in plastic bags and then into a small, unlabeled box that was in turn put inside a darkroom sink! I found the box a year later, after having spent hours at the hardware store and about $60 replacing the nuts, bolts and shelf supports.

—*FARRON D. BROUGHER*
ANAHEIM, CALIFORNIA
🚚 *4 MOVES*

• • • • • • • • •

DURING ONE OF MY MOVES, I put all of my very expensive pieces of art in one package. And, of course, that one package went missing. I'll never do that again.

—*EMMILLIO E.*
VANCOUVER, BRITISH COLUMBIA, CANADA
🚚 *7 MOVES*

• • • • • • • • •

THERE ARE TWO THINGS I'VE LOST while moving that I'll always regret: my patched jeans from high school and my Elton John concert T-shirt. They just disappeared. When you pack up, you'd better find the things you love and put them in a safe place first.

—*RUTH CORNETT*
LANSING, MICHIGAN
🚚 *10 MOVES*

WE MOVED FAR AWAY, in December, with two kids who were in the middle of their school years. On top of all the other adjustments, we were building a new house and it wasn't ready, so we moved into a hotel. We had adjoining rooms but only one bathroom, which added to the challenge. We also had no kitchen, so we had to eat out all the time. It was amazingly stressful.

—*ANONYMOUS*
WAKEFIELD, NEW HAMPSHIRE
10 MOVES

. . . .

THE WORST PLACE I EVER MOVED into was a dilapidated apartment with a permanently mildewed carpet in downtown Concord, California. There was no air conditioning, so in the summer, the only relief was to open the windows. But the place was right behind Hobie's Roadhouse, which played blues until 2 a.m. Then I got to hear a bunch of people leave the bar in a drunken stupor. I lived there a year—it seemed like ten!

—*ALLAN JAFFE*
PETALUMA, CALIFORNIA

. . . .

I SPENT A LOT OF MY TIME as a young mother sewing baby clothes for my youngest child. I had all the clothes I made and a few special outfits from family in a box and I remember on the day of the move, a mover was admiring them and complimented me on my work. He told me that he had to repack the items in a special moving box. He also mentioned that his wife was pregnant. When we arrived, the box was gone. I still think about it to this day, 12 years later.

—*BONNIE LAMB*
CHICAGO, ILLINOIS

THINK TWICE BEFORE YOU MOVE into a place that you haven't seen with your own eyes! When I was a newlywed, my husband and I relocated to Killeen, Texas. I was shocked to learn that our apartment was connected to another apartment through a small bathroom—which both families were expected to share. It wasn't long before I got tired of the man next door smoking in the restroom, leaving ashes in the sink, and blaming it on us when his wife complained!

—*ANNA ANDERSON*
BARLING, ARKANSAS
3 MOVES

• • • • • • • •

DON'T OVERREACT IF YOU THINK your moving truck is gone. When we moved from California to Montana, nobody could locate ours for a couple of days, which left me in a daze. I mean, how can you misplace a whole truck full of furniture? Fortunately, 48 hours later, we got a phone call. Our truck was being stored in an out-of-town facility about 300 miles away, because the town we moved to didn't have any storage space. They apologized profusely and brought the truck over as soon as possible.

—*JOAN K. HITCHENS*
CENTENNIAL, COLORADO
3 MOVES

Moving is one of the most stressful times in a person's life.

—*U-HAUL*

• • • • • • • •

EVERY TIME YOU DON'T THINK YOU HAVE as much as the Jones's, try moving it. I thought I could move all our stuff in one truck. By the end of the day, we had a truck, a trailer and two station wagons filled with stuff.

—*J.K. DAPRATO*
VANCOUVER, WASHINGTON

ONCE, MY EX-BOYFRIEND AND I decided to move into an apartment together. It took me 2 weeks to move in all of my stuff. A year later, things went south. What had taken me 2 weeks and 10 carloads to get into the apartment took me a sum total of 15 minutes to move out. I think it was the fastest spring cleaning I had ever done.

—MAJA GERDIN
SAN ANTONIO, TEXAS
10 MOVES

• • • • • • • •

I MOVED ONCE JUST SIX BLOCKS AWAY. No problem, I figured. But it was a sweltering July afternoon, and I couldn't track down anybody with a truck in time to haul the big things out. So there I was, stumbling down the street with a desk on my back, nearly collapsing from the heat (and the desk). I had to stop no fewer than 20 times during the arduous journey. Now I make a more concerted effort to locate a truck beforehand.

—J.A.
LOS ANGELES, CALIFORNIA
7 MOVES

• • • • • • • •

I MOVED FROM BALTIMORE, MARYLAND, to the Bay Area in California for a new career with a new company. That move was harder than any other because I effectively left what I knew behind me and headed for the unknown. Ultimately, it was one of the most rewarding choices I have ever made because it allowed me to get to know myself and strengthen aspects of my personality that really needed work.

—DON DASHER
SARATOGA, CALIFORNIA
10 MOVES

GOOD ON THE BACK, BAD ON THE LEGS

My wife, ever the innovative one, decided to move our stuff in about 1,000 little plastic shopping bags, instead of boxes. She thought it would be better on my back. What she didn't take into consideration was whether it would be better on my legs.

I began carrying little bags down at 8 a.m. Nine hours later, my legs trembling like two brittle reeds, I gave up, crawled into the rental truck, and drove to the new place. There were still, perhaps, another 200 little bags to move out of our old apartment. Since I'd already left for the new place (hoping to put my legs in ice water, or hot water, or perhaps a bucket of scotch), my wife finished the move with her mother's help.

Now, my wife's mother, who's even more innovative than her daughter, and in terrific shape, bounded lightly up the stairs, took one look at the situation, and ran a 100-foot line out the window. She attached a wicker basket to the line, and started lowering little shopping bags to the sidewalk 80 feet below. I'm not kidding. I think my wife gets her sense of innovation from her father.

—RICHARD G. CALO
EAGLE BRIDGE, NEW YORK
15 MOVES

WE MOVED DURING A BLIZZARD. I had no choice—we had to be out of my old place by midnight. The later it got, the harder it snowed. It was brutal. We could barely see what we were doing or where we were going as we carried stuff from the house to the truck. More than one thing broke, I can tell you that. The next day I slept until noon.

—*MARTIN SEABECK*
FOMBELL, PENNSYLVANIA
7 MOVES

· · · · · · · ·

" My bicycle was mangled, my mattress was torn, glass was shattered, and wood was coming off my table in shreds. I sued the movers, but only received $200, from which I had to pay the lawyers' fees. "

—*L.K.*
NASHVILLE, TENNESSEE
8 MOVES

· · · · · · · ·

OUR MOVER INJURED HIS HAND and asked someone else to complete the drive for him. Our belongings didn't arrive. The mover's friend got drunk and left the truck at a rest stop.

—*C.F.*
LIBERTYVILLE, ILLINOIS
8 MOVES

ALWAYS GET THE INSURANCE when you're driving something unfamiliar. I did it only because I was completely hung over at the time and wasn't thinking. But when, in my foggy haze, I parked in the alleyway of a one-way street, I crashed into the building, and the side mirror snapped off and shattered on the sidewalk. Fortunately, this incident only cost me $20—the price of the insurance. Without the policy, it would've been at least $200. Even if you're sober, something's bound to happen.

> —*LIBBY DEBLASIO*
> *DENVER, COLORADO*
> 7 *MOVES*

• • • • • • • •

I WAS THRILLED TO DISCOVER that my new apartment had crickets, which I took as a sign of good luck until a friend of mine said, "You may call those crickets, but where I come from we call them cockroaches."

> —*MARTHA ENGLERT*
> *MADISON, WISCONSIN*

• • • • • • • •

I FOUND OUT THAT I HAD TO HAVE emergency dental surgery the day we moved. We had rented a truck that my girlfriend refused to drive, and I couldn't, because my face was blown up like a balloon, and I was on all kinds of painkillers. At the last minute my girlfriend talked a friend of hers into driving us to New York City. When we got there, I was half asleep on the floor in between the two of them. We ended up having to drive all the way down Second Avenue for miles, and it was rush hour. We didn't hit anything, but that's a miracle.

> —*RYAN*
> *DURHAM, NORTH CAROLINA*
> 11 *MOVES*

Don't forget to transfer all your insurance policies to your new town.

> —*THE UNOFFICIAL GUIDE TO BUYING A HOME*

WORST MOVE EVER: We went to pick up the rental truck in the early afternoon. The clerk was typing with one finger. It took forever. Then the computer froze, and she had to start over. We finally got a truck and it wouldn't start. They gave us another one. The engine light was on. We drove away. It was loud and sounded awful. At one point, the brake light went off, too. When we got to my old place, the truck got stuck in the snow. It took about 30 minutes to get it unstuck. On the way to my new place, the passenger door wouldn't stay closed. When we got there, the lights wouldn't stay on. So, we unloaded in the dark. I had everything so planned, but everything went wrong.

—*DEBBIE L.*
CAMILLUS, NEW YORK
11 MOVES

Last Chance: What to Do Before You Move In

N*ot everyone has the option of doing major work to their new place before they move in. After all, you need a roof over your head, and you won't be able to use yours if you're renovating beneath it. Still, we asked movers the question: If you could do one thing to your house before you moved in, what would it be? Read on, and plan accordingly.*

SPEND AT LEAST ONE NIGHT IN YOUR PLACE before unpacking. Get a feel for it so you can think about how you'd want it all laid out. Then maybe you won't have to set up twice.

—Z.K.
MINNEAPOLIS, MINNESOTA
5 MOVES

CLEAN EVERY-THING FIRST.

—ROBYN
BIGLERVILLE,
PENNSYLVANIA
4 MOVES

RE-DO HARDWOOD FLOORS, install carpeting, and paint walls *before* you move in.

—*J.W.*
ROCHESTER, NEW YORK
14 MOVES

• • • • • • • •

IF YOU HAVE HARDWOOD FLOORS, make sure to get the walls ready beforehand so you don't have to move furniture around and scratch them while you paint.

—*C.L.*
MINNEAPOLIS, MINNESOTA
2 MOVES

• • • • • • • •

KILL ALL THE BUGS IN YOUR STUFF before you move—don't take them with you. We moved from South America to Iowa and I brought beautiful wooden products, crawling with termites. They infected all of Iowa. Also, I bought these beautiful tapestries made by a famous local artist that had moths. I had to throw the wooden things away, but I froze the tapestries in the Iowa winter to keep them.

—SUSAN LANSHE ESCOBAR
SAN ANTONIO, TEXAS
5 MOVES

• • • • • • • •

TAKE THE MOVE-IN DAMAGE REPORT sheet seriously, and get everything in writing! When we moved into our first apartment, which was brand-new, I noticed the bathroom flooring had been installed incorrectly, leaving a huge gap by the bathtub. Management said they'd fix it, but this never got done. Over the years, water damage caused the flooring to tear up. When we moved out, they sent us a $250 bill to pay for the replacement flooring *and* they kept our deposit!

—RACHEL WALASKAY
SEDALIA, COLORADO
3 MOVES

For to-do lists, put the 80/20 principle to work—make sure only 20 percent of the items on your list are a priority at any one time.

—*THE ONE-MINUTE ORGANIZER*

MAKE SURE YOUR APPLIANCES WILL FIT where you want them. Measure everything ahead of time, especially if you are buying new stuff. We found that we couldn't put our refrigerator where the last family had it because ours was too high. To put it on the other side of the kitchen involved taking out some cabinets—and that was no fun at all.

—BRANDON BUCKLEY
YOUNGSTOWN, PENNSYLVANIA
3 MOVES

Always replace the toilet seat.

—TIM SMITH
MINNEAPOLIS, MINNESOTA
3 MOVES

. . . .

When you get to your new home, before you move anything in or unpack, take a roll full of pictures. It's fascinating to look back on how the place looked before you painted, decorated, and renovated.

—JENNIFER BRIGHT REICH
HELLERTOWN, PENNSYLVANIA
6 MOVES

. . . .

CLEAN YOUR NEW PLACE BEFORE you move in. Get all that silly work done. My wife painted all four rooms downstairs and I redid the floors in the bedrooms, too. If you paint after you move in, you've got to cover all the furniture and stuff. It's easiest if all that stuff isn't there yet.

—ROY
WAUWATOSA, WISCONSIN
4 MOVES

ONE NIGHT, SHORTLY AFTER MOVING into an apartment, we came home from work and our entire basement apartment had been flooded. There was about six inches of water on the floor, and everything we had (basically, our clothes) was ruined. It was a good lesson for us: ALWAYS GET RENTERS' INSURANCE. Seriously, it's so cheap, maybe $100 a year for $50,000 worth of coverage.

—ALANA WATKINS
DENVER, COLORADO
5 MOVES

• • • • • • • •

WALK THROUGH THE PROPERTY and document on paper everything that's damaged. I don't care how minute you think it is—a nick in the wall, a chip on a tile, a crack in the ceiling;—everything should be written down. This is true whether you're renting or buying a place. If you're renting, your damage deposit is at stake. If you're buying, you might get stuck with costly repairs in the future if you don't bring potential damage to the proper attention now.

—P.O.
NEW BRUNSWICK, NEW JERSEY
6 MOVES

• • • • • • • •

Brighten up or change your new home's look with a fresh coat of paint.

—A.O.
LAGUNA HILLS,
CALIFORNIA
4 MOVES

BOTH TIMES I'VE MOVED I've been lucky enough to move into vacant homes. So I had the great luxury of being able to paint, wallpaper, and clean before I moved and then I could move my things in little by little.

—Z.
HELLERTOWN, PENNSYLVANIA
2 MOVES

WE MOVED IN ON A STEAMY HOT JUNE DAY in downtown Atlanta, only to find that the prior tenants had left the house in utter filth. The refrigerator and freezer housed an army of cockroaches who apparently found refuge from the heat in our soon-to-be-at-the-dump appliance. The place was just plain unsanitary. Luckily we found the strength to clean at least one space . . . the bathroom. It was a good choice because after the stress of closing on our first mortgage, the excitement of moving in with my life partner, and facing the immense task of renovating a 100-year-old Craftsman bungalow, I spent the greater part of my first day in my new home throwing up.

—*LYNN YOFFEE*
TALKING ROCK, GEORGIA
20 MOVES

• • • • • • • •

HAVE YOUR NEW HOUSE EXTERMINATED before you move in. That's the only time the chemicals can get into every nook and cranny without damaging your stuff.

—*JOE HOLLIMAN*
CENTENNIAL, COLORADO
2 MOVES

• • • • • • • •

MOVE INTO A SPOTLESS SPACE. It truly makes a difference.

—*JILL*
WEEHAWKEN, NEW JERSEY
12 MOVES

Don't try to live through renovations with little kids. It's dangerous and miserable.

—*DANIELA*
CORTE MADERA, CALIFORNIA
6 MOVES

If you have allergies, take your pills before you clean your house!

—*MICHAEL*
SANTA MONICA,
CALIFORNIA
20 MOVES

WHEN WE MOVED INTO A NEW CONSTRUCTION, we made sure they washed all the windows and skylights when they were done. But we learned something important: You have to wash skylights from the outside. When they did ours, they removed the skylight from the inside and then washed it. They didn't re-secure it properly and we ended up with a lot of outside noise. If we hadn't caught the problem, we would have had leaks all winter.

—*M.J.W.*
KIRKLAND, WASHINGTON
4 MOVES

* * * * * * * *

" Make sure you have a key from the landlord before moving in. Otherwise you may come back at 2 a.m. only to find he has locked all the doors, and you have no way to get in or contact him. "

—*KEVIN K.*
CROWN POINT, INDIANA

* * * * * * * *

IF YOU'RE GOING TO PAINT OR WALLPAPER, do it before you move all your stuff in. We unpacked everything and then had to move our stuff into the center of the room and back. It was so stupid.

—*TALLIE FISHBURNE*
MINNEAPOLIS, MINNESOTA
7 MOVES

GET THE MEASUREMENTS

ALWAYS MAKE SURE THE THINGS YOU WANT to move will fit into your new place. I had to get rid of a queen-size bed because I realized—while I was moving—that it wouldn't fit up the stairs.

> —HOLLY MOORE
> SAN DIEGO, CALIFORNIA

• • • • • • • • •

ASK YOUR APARTMENT COMPLEX for floor plan drawings, which show the rooms and their sizes.

> —ELOISE MILLIKEN
> CALIFON, NEW JERSEY
> 12 MOVES

• • • • • • • • •

MAKE SURE YOU MEASURE THE BIG FURNITURE and the doors and hallways of your new place. My dad had to saw an entertainment center in half, move the parts into the TV room, and then glue it back together. And another time, I was there to move my then-fiancé out of his apartment. I have no idea how he got his couch in, but when it came time to move it out, the movers just couldn't get it through the door. They ended up having to lower it off a second story balcony with ropes.

> —JEN W.
> SAN CARLOS, CALIFORNIA
> 3 MOVES

DO ALL THE RENOVATIONS YOU CAN to your home *before* you move in. Once you move in and unpack, forget it! Small things like a piece of trim missing from a wall aren't impairments to living, so you never get around to doing them.

—*ANONYMOUS*
SHOEMAKERSVILLE, PENNSYLVANIA
1 MOVE

• • • • • • • •

GET YOUR FLOORS REFINISHED or re-carpeted before you move in. Otherwise, you'll have to deal with the hassle of moving furniture out of the way. Plus, you might have to spend a few nights in a hotel while the polyurethane dries.

—*JULIE MARTIN SUNICH*
TAMPA, FLORIDA
12 MOVES

• • • • • • • •

To help organize your new home, you can hire a local professional organizer through the National Association of Professional Organizers.

—*WWW.NAPO.NET*

SET ASIDE MONEY FOR DECORATING the new place. We used security deposits from other places to decorate the new place. We bought stuff for the kitchen, posters, a mirror and stuff for the living room.

—*VANESSA*
MILWAUKEE, WISCONSIN
5 MOVES

• • • • • • • •

TAKE ALL THE INSIDE DOORS OFF THEIR HINGES and stack them in the basement. More often than not you are going to run into a situation where something doesn't want to go into the room and the door needs to be removed. It's much easier to do that first, while you know where your tools are, than to try to find that stuff in the middle of the move.

—*TORREY MATUSEV*
YOUNGSTOWN, PENNSYLVANIA
4 MOVES

I **LIVED IN ONE PLACE THAT** I swear was haunted. Doors were always slamming shut and stuff was always moved around. You might want to have an exorcist go through any places you're thinking about renting.

—*E.G.*
ACCIDENT, MARYLAND
2 MOVES

• • • • • • • •

Call a week ahead of time and make sure electricity will be turned on and the High Definition cable installer will be there the day you move in. Gas, water, garbage, and phone are all optional as long as you have ESPN in High Definition on Day One.

—*J.S.*
EDINA, MINNESOTA
5 MOVES

• • • • • • • •

ANY EXISTING WALLPAPER in your new place needs to be replaced whether it's in good shape or not. Unlike paint, wallpaper is your personal statement about a room. It tells people something about your personality.

—*J.J.*
BULGER, PENNSYLVANIA
2 MOVES

ADVICE FOR PEOPLE WHO THINK they should pull up carpeting themselves: Pay someone else to do it! It is a major project and is well worth the expense to have a professional do it for you.

—*STEVEN MACKAY*
SAN FRANCISCO, CALIFORNIA
MOVED TOO MANY TIMES

• • • • • • • •

TAKE CARE OF THE URGENT THINGS FIRST, and do it before you move in. Paint and lay down the rugs before you bring in the furniture.

—*K. BECKERING*
SYRACUSE, NEW YORK
4 MOVES

• • • • • • • •

THE MOST IMPORTANT THING TO DO is to call the utility companies to get the process started. It usually takes a while to get service from the gas, electric, phone, cable and garbage collection companies. Don't wait.

—*BRIAN HORZICH*
WHEELING, WEST VIRGINIA
5 MOVES

First Things First: Getting Unpacked

Y ou're in! The couch made it to the living room, and the paint has all dried. Now comes the next hurdle—unpacking all those boxes and deciding where everything goes. But before you find yourself knee-deep in packing peanuts, wondering where in the world you put the bottle opener, read this chapter. Unpacking is an art form. Do it right, and you will soon feel at home. Do it wrong, and you have a mess.

WHEN YOU FIRST MOVE IN, immediately place the boxes in the center of the rooms they go in. If they're in your way, it forces you to sort through them quickly. It only takes me about three days to completely unpack this way.

—L.E.
POMONA, CALIFORNIA
16 MOVES

I UNPACK MY CATS. THEN, MY STEREO.

—J.A.
DURHAM,
NORTH CAROLINA
16 MOVES

PACK A COOLER WITH BASICS FOR EATING. It stinks to wake up in your new home and not have milk for your coffee when you're not sure where the nearest grocery store is.

—*JILL MARIE DAVIS*
WEEHAWKEN, NEW JERSEY
12 MOVES

• • • • • • • •

WE MOVED IN ON A FRIDAY, and we had company coming on Saturday, so I was forced to unpack the entire house in one day. This CAN be done! I put the kitchen together first, and arranged all of our furniture. Boxes full of miscellaneous stuff that we didn't have time to unpack, I put in the basement.

—*L.A.*
CLEVELAND, OHIO
11 MOVES

• • • • • • • •

The kitchen is the room to unpack first. I'm always hungry.

—*JACQUELINE*
MCKEOWN
SAN DIEGO,
CALIFORNIA
5 MOVES

I WAS IN SUCH A MANIC STATE that I unpacked throughout the entire night that I arrived. I was so ready to be somewhere else. I stayed up all night long and unpacked and put everything away. In the morning, I was in my new house, all set up. It was great.

—*NANCY*
PORTLAND, MAINE
8 MOVES

• • • • • • • •

THE WORST PART OF MOVING IS that while you are helping your dad move the heavy stuff, your mom, in her boredom or desire to be helpful, will unpack all of your little stuff. It took me a week to find my contact lenses.

—*AARON MUNSON*
INDIANAPOLIS, INDIANA

UNPACKING IS ALWAYS A CHORE and something that seems to be put off forever in my house. In an attempt to change things, I scheduled a large house-warming party for about one or two weeks after the close on our new house. Talk about incentive to have things looking perfect. The house was 95 percent unpacked by the start of the party and has remained the same ever since.

—*DON DASHER*
SARATOGA, CALIFORNIA
10 MOVES

· · · · · · · ·

" I still have things in boxes from when my husband and I moved into our condo four years ago. If you don't unpack things right away, you'll never get to them. "

—*JEAN ROBERTSON*
GLENVIEW, ILLINOIS
3 MOVES

· · · · · · · ·

DON'T TRY TO DO EVERYTHING AT ONCE. If you have lots of boxes to unpack, just understand that it's going to take a while. My husband and I had to go right back to work after the move. We didn't have the luxury of taking time off to unpack. So we picked one room each evening to work on. It's much less daunting if you have a realistic goal to shoot for.

—*VALERIE SHUSTECK*
YOUNGSTOWN, PENNSYLVANIA
2 MOVES

WAIT A WHILE BEFORE YOU RENOVATE. When you first buy a place and move in, you're full of ideas and energy, and it may seem like the best time to get stuff done. But you will soon discover that the way you live in the house is different from what you expected. Your renovation ideas will change and you'll end up with something much better for your real lifestyle.

—TONY
CHICAGO, ILLINOIS
5 MOVES

• • • • • • • • •

USE A NEW DECORATING SCHEME in your new living room. Use colors that you've never used before. Set up the furniture in a way that you've never done before. Be creative. A new start calls for changes.

—JOAN PIERSON
CRANBERRY TOWNSHIP, PENNSYLVANIA
2 MOVES

'CAN YOU SPARE A SQUARE?'

WHAT TO UNPACK FIRST: toilet paper. It's a necessity.

—ALYSSA AGEE
SNOQUALMIE, WASHINGTON
10 MOVES

• • • • • • • • •

HAVE TOILET PAPER ON HAND BEFORE ANYTHING ELSE. I drove over to help a friend move in and she had all these boxes with no toilet paper. Luckily I had just been to Costco and busted out a few rolls. Everyone was so happy—I saved the day.

—KELLEY HOFFNER
DENVER, COLORADO
7 MOVES

MY GOAL IS TO GET TOTALLY UNPACKED within a week, because I find that after that, I don't want to deal with it anymore and things tend to stay the way they are. The house kind of gels around me and it seems to take a major effort to do anything else to it.

—*JOANNE WOLFE*
NESKOWIN, OREGON
34 MOVES

• • • • • • • •

❝ You have to get the food and beer in the fridge so you can feed the people who helped you move. Everything else can wait. ❞

—*MARY WEBB*
WHEELING, WEST VIRGINIA
4 MOVES

• • • • • • • •

NOTHING CAN BE MORE CHAOTIC than trying to feel at home in your new digs. Keep necessities boxed nearby: towels, soap, toilet paper, toothpaste and brush, coffee pot and cups and two or more place settings of dishes. Whatever your family loves the most, try to have on hand. This will make you feel more at home from the start.

—*JANIS BLAISE*
DIABLO, CALIFORNIA
16 MOVES

SET UP THE LIVING ROOM FIRST. Hook up the TV and stereo, and set the couch down. These items will come in handy when you need a place to eat and relax. Plus, you can have some music to unpack to.

—*A.D.*
HARRINGTON, MAINE
🚚 *2 MOVES*

· · · · · · · ·

" Set up your bedroom first because, by the end of the night, you'll be so exhausted that you'll want a bed to sleep in. "

—*KATHARENE JOHNSON*
RIDGECREST, CALIFORNIA
🚚 *10 MOVES*

· · · · · · · ·

MY RULE OF THUMB IS to put up your art first. Get the walls decorated and make it feel like home; then do the rest.

—*SCOTT STEVENS*
PORTLAND, OREGON
🚚 *3 MOVES*

· · · · · · · ·

WE ALWAYS UNPACKED BED LINENS and towels very early in the move. A telephone is essential to start out your life in your new home. And if you don't want to spend exorbitant amounts of money eating in restaurants in the beginning, unpack some kitchen utensils so you can do some simple cooking.

—*KAZ BROWNLEE*
VANCOUVER, BRITISH COLUMBIA, CANADA
🚚 *30 MOVES*

☆
After you unpack for a while, crack a drink, and just relax.

—*ANONYMOUS*
BIRMINGHAM, ALABAMA
🚚 *7 MOVES*

HOME IS WHERE THE ACCIDENTS HAPPEN

Moving into my very first house after years of renting was such an overwhelming yet exciting experience. When I walked in the door for the first time, I didn't want to touch anything. I wanted everything to stay new, untouched and unworn. I was afraid to shut the doors too hard, open the windows too fast, even walk around with shoes on! I did really well the first few days—picking up after myself, avoiding rooms with white carpet. I finally learned to let my guard down after my dog had an accident on the floor, and I realized that you can't live in a house without it eventually looking "lived in." Hardwood floors are going to get scratched. Carpets will get stained. Pets will have accidents. Once I relaxed and accepted wear and tear for what it was, it finally started to feel like a home.

—*CELESTE DODGE*
WALTHAM, MASSCHUSETTS
7 MOVES

UNPACK AT YOUR DESTINATION as soon as possible to get things back to normal and decrease the stress for you and the rest of your family. Familiarity makes moving easier.

—*J.M. CORNWELL*
TABERNASH, COLORADO
11 MOVES

. . . .

" Surround yourself with familiar things like pictures of friends and family right away. "

—*TOM FISHBURNE*
MINNEAPOLIS, MINNESOTA
7 MOVES

. . . .

WHAT TO UNPACK FIRST? For a Brit, cups, kettle, bottle opener and glasses are key, followed by plates for the inevitable pizza! I do it every time, and I never regret it.

—*A.M.*
CAMBRIDGE, MASSACHUSETTS

. . . .

Unpack your liquor first. Get the booze out and set your stereo up. Make it fun.

—*K.B.*
DIABLO,
CALIFORNIA
16 MOVES

PACK UP YOUR CHILDREN'S STUFF LAST and unpack it first. We wanted to make sure everything in our son's room was set up—his favorite toys out, his bed ready for a nap. Children find moving just as stressful as adults, at any age, so we always try to minimize the stress.

—*VANESSA WILKINSON*
COLORA, MARYLAND
6 MOVES

I UNPACK MY STEREO AND CDS FIRST so I have music for unpacking the rest of my boxes. It helps me settle in and creates a sense of familiarity in a new place.

—*NICOLE HOWARD*
SEATTLE, WASHINGTON
6 MOVES

• • • • • • • •

MY KITCHEN AND BATHROOM get set up first, because I need to start cooking immediately and I need to access bath items fairly quickly. The other stuff can wait.

—*EMPISH THOMAS*
ATLANTA, GEORGIA
7 MOVES

• • • • • • • •

COMPUTER AND STEREO are always the first things to set up. Music makes the rest of the process much more tolerable, and the computer is just essential to my lifestyle.

—*ALLEN R. PYLE*
HILLSDALE, MICHIGAN
6 MOVES

• • • • • • • •

WHEN I UNPACK, I like to be able to prepare something to eat, give someone a call, see if the ISP actually got my hook-up going and have a comfy place to crash at the end of that exhausting day.

—*ANNETTE C. YOUNG*
VANCOUVER, WASHINGTON
8 MOVES

• • • • • • • •

WHEN MOVING, I UNPACK THE LIVING ROOM first. I unpack the TV and couch because that's the main room and if you have people helping you move then they'll have a place to relax and take a break.

—*D.A.*
CHICAGO, ILLINOIS
4 MOVES

GROOVE OFF, MOVE STILL ON

I moved from New York City to Boulder, Colorado—places that are different in pretty much every respect. My first night in Boulder, I was determined to make friends. I went to a popular hotspot wearing all black and ordered a martini in a tumbler glass. Then I hit the dance floor to get my groove on. On the dance floor, a guy with dreadlocks was dancing so intensely that one of his dreads broke off and fell into my martini. As my drink started to fizz, I burst into tears. I ran outside and called United Airlines to book me on a flight out of Boulder. Alas, there were no more flights to New York that evening. I sat on the curb and cried some more. Eventually, I remembered why I'd moved. I went back inside and  ordered another martini. I stayed in Boulder for two more years. Remember that first impressions aren't always accurate. You have to give a place at least six months before it begins to feel like home. And one more thing: Don't order a martini at a jam-band bar.

    —AMANDA J.

GET ALL YOUR "ACCESSORIES"—like pictures, paintings and other decorations—put in place as quick as you can. You'll be surprised how quickly you'll feel at home when you have these familiar pieces of yours to look at.

> —*DENISE LABATOS*
> *YOUNGSTOWN, PENNSYLVANIA*
> 🚚 *4 MOVES*

· · · · · · · ·

" Open every box. Resist the temptation to just store that box in the garage. Out of sight, out of mind. "

> —*DARIN WATKINS*
> *PALOUSE, WASHINGTON*
> 🚚 *20 MOVES*

· · · · · · · ·

SHEETS AND TOWELS, so everyone can shower easily. Feeling clean helps you face a day of unpacking.

> —*ELIZABETH BONET*
> *SUNRISE, FLORIDA*
> 🚚 *13 MOVES*

· · · · · · · ·

THE LAST TIME I MOVED I found some boxes in my bedroom closet that had never been unpacked from my previous move. I had to open them up to see what the heck they were. It was a bunch of junk from childhood that my mom had saved and given to me. I threw it all right in the trash. If you find stuff that you haven't even looked at for that long don't bother unpacking it.

> —*R.G.*
> *PITTSBURGH, PENNSYLVANIA*
> 🚚 *3 MOVES*

NEVER UNDERESTIMATE HOW MUCH TIME it will take to unpack. If you're moving to a new town and starting a new job, postpone the starting date for a day, week or month so your house and life are set up before your job.

—A.D.
MINNEAPOLIS, MINNESOTA
4 MOVES

Put on music! Empty houses or apartments are too spooky-quiet.

—*JOHN PLATT*
SOMERSET,
NEW JERSEY
4 MOVES

I LIKE TO PUT UP PICTURES and personal knick-knacks as soon as possible—it helps me to see familiar things in my new place, and get a quick start to feeling "at home."

—*SANDRA A.*
MARIETTA, GEORGIA
6 MOVES

MOVING IS TOTAL CHAOS. In order to feel like we had some sense of control, we decided ahead of time on locations for some key things that we didn't want to misplace—namely our keys, wallets, and medications. That way, even if everything else was in chaos, we knew where those important items were.

—*JON*
BIGLERVILLE, PENNSYLVANIA
4 MOVES

WE SET UP OUR BOOKCASES in the living room and unpacked our books first. For us, there just wasn't a greater gesture or symbol of permanency. All the other boxes and rooms had to wait. We could hear all the wooden spoons in the kitchen squeal in unison from their box, "Unpack us and cook something!" but we told them, "You just have to wait!"

—*EDGAR POMA*
SAN FRANCISCO, CALIFORNIA
2 MOVES

DEFINITE DON'TS FOR THE NEWLY ARRIVED

NOT THAT I HAVE EVER DONE THESE THINGS, of course, but if you have recently moved into a new place, you should avoid the following in order to comfortably settle into your new neighborhood:

• **PRACTICING NAKED YOGA** at night, in front of your window, with the blinds open

• **LEAVING YOUR TRASH CAN OUT** for three days following trash pick-up

• **LETTING YOUR DOG POOP** in the neighbor's yard . . . and leaving it there

• **WATCHING THE NEIGHBORS** through the permanent peephole in your blinds

• **LEAVING YOUR DOG** in the yard all day, letting him constantly bark at everything

—*H.N.*
OKLAHOMA CITY, OKLAHOMA
7 MOVES

PUT TOGETHER THE KITCHEN FIRST so you can make tea or coffee for the moving men. They'll be so grateful that they'll work harder, faster, and more carefully. I managed to get the moving men to start putting away the linens and making the beds this way. Once they even played with the children!

—*F.T.L.*
METZ, FRANCE
4 MOVES

• • • • • • • •

" **My first room is the laundry room. I have four children. My washer and dryer are like my right arm.** "

—*N.E.*
HOUSTON, TEXAS
MOVED TO EUROPE

• • • • • • • •

MAKE SURE TO SET UP THE BEDROOM and the kitchen so you have a place to sleep and make tea.

—*C.K.*
FALMOUTH, MAINE
2 MOVES

• • • • • • • •

THE FIRST FEW WEEKS CAN BE INTIMIDATING and overwhelming because there is just so damn much to do. Make yourself a reasonable to-do list each day and stick rigidly to it. Make sure you allow enough time in your daily schedule to unwind and enjoy your new place.

—*PAULA GRUBBS*
RENFREW, PENNSYLVANIA
3 MOVES

THE MOST IMPORTANT ROOM to set up is the family room. It really is the most important room in the house. It's the entertainment room, the dining room, and a sanctuary, all rolled up into one. It's the place where the whole family can spend time together, which is essential after a big move.

—*LEIGH DOBSON*
TORONTO, ONTARIO, CANADA
14 MOVES

• • • • • • • •

I KNOW A LOT OF PEOPLE DON'T LIKE to have their moms arranging their homes, but there is something to be said for having her completely unpack and organize the kitchen.

—*CHELI BROWN*
ATLANTA, GEORGIA
10 MOVES

• • • • • • • •

THE KITCHEN COMES FIRST. I have three small kids and feeding them is important.

—*BART G. FARKAS*
COCHRANE, ALBERTA, CANADA
8 MOVES

• • • • • • • •

I HIRED MY CLEANING LADY to come the day after my move and help me unpack. Having a professional—or even just a very organized friend—to help pack or unpack is invaluable. That person isn't emotionally attached to your belongings like you are. They'll keep you from oohing and aahing over every photo, book, and piece of clothing that you unpack and keep you on track until everything's put away.

—*ELLEN*
PITTSBURGH, PENNSYLVANIA
11 MOVES

Within 24 hours of moving, take a break from the rearranging and unpacking to enjoy a leisure activity with the family—one that's different from what you did at your old home.

—*APARTMENTS.COM*

DON'T TAKE 10 YEARS TO UNPACK those boxes. They will take up your whole garage. Even if you can only make yourself do one a month, you will be way ahead of the game. The only advantage to waiting is that when you get around to it you can throw away most of the stuff you find inside. The books are out of date, the clothes have been outgrown, and the children are too old for the toys.

—*LINDA REEVES*
SAN ANTONIO, TEXAS
15 MOVES

• • • • • • • • •

NO MATTER WHAT STAGE OF UNPACKING you are at by the day's end, have a drink to calm your nerves before you go to sleep.

—*JENNIFER ROGERS*
UPSTATE NEW YORK

• • • • • • • •

I MADE SURE THAT WE PACKED one room at a time, and unpacked everything the same way. That part of the process worked out quite well, and I certainly would recommend that to anyone moving from one house to another.

—*L. RANALLI*
DREXEL HILL, PENNSYLVANIA
5 MOVES

• • • • • • • • •

YOU NEED TO CONSIDER all of those damn empty boxes. Movers will make one return trip as part of their service, but unless you wait until all of the boxes are emptied, you'll be stuck with a mountain of them to recycle or discard. If the movers unpack, the boxes will be emptied and out of your life in a day.

—*FARRON D. BROUGHER*
ANAHEIM, CALIFORNIA
4 MOVES

UNPACK ALL YOUR BOXES within a week of moving in. It's too easy to only unpack the necessities and leave everything else for later. But "later" becomes three months later, and you still have spare rooms full of boxes.

—*J.S.*
EDINA, MINNESOTA
5 MOVES

. . . .

Avoid getting drunk and making a fool of yourself in front of the new neighbors the first day. That can wait at least a week.

—*PAM SASSER*
WHEELING, WEST VIRGINIA
4 MOVES

. . . .

I LIKE TO MAKE SURE THE BEDS are set up first. A good night's sleep is high on my priority list.

—*ANONYMOUS*
PETALUMA, CALIFORNIA
3 MOVES

. . . .

QUICKLY PUT your own stamp on the new place. Shortly after moving, I set up my favorite posters on the wall so that it felt like my own room.

—*CHRISTIAN BATOG*
FRANKLIN, MASSACHUSETTS
6 MOVES

MAKE SURE YOUR LANDSCAPING looks great immediately. This is a big deal to the rest of the neighborhood. What happens inside your home is your business, but the outside matters to everybody else, so take care of that first.

—*EMMILLIO E.*
VANCOUVER, BRITISH COLUMBIA, CANADA
🚚 *7 MOVES*

• • • • • • • •

I ALWAYS TELL PEOPLE TO EXPECT to spend twice as long unpacking as it takes you to pack.

—*M.E.S.*
CARNEGIE, PENNSYLVANIA
🚚 *8 MOVES*

Settling In: Make Yourself at Home

Your new place is the best! Your new place is awful! You absolutely love the neighborhood! You feel like a complete outcast! And where in the world is the closest Wal-Mart? If you can relate to any of this angst, it sounds like you're just starting to settle in. Sure, it takes time. But sooner or later, you'll find all your favorite places, you'll meet the neighbors, and you'll no longer get lost three blocks from home. Here are some tips to help you get there.

GO FOR LOTS OF WALKS. That's how my husband and I met a lot of our neighbors. It also helped us get a lay of the land. We had a housewarming party, but we met more people passing out invitations than we did at the actual party.

—*L.O.*
SYRACUSE, NEW YORK
5 MOVES

MOVING IS EASY—IT'S THE SETTLING DOWN THAT'S DIFFICULT.

—*JON G.*
LONDON, ENGLAND
3 MOVES

WHEN YOU MOVE, try to remember that *everything* in your life may feel out of whack for the first three months or so.

—*SHELLEY*
PHILADELPHIA, PENNSYLVANIA
3 MOVES

• • • • • • • •

GET TO KNOW THE KIDS in your neighborhood—especially if you're computer illiterate, like I am. There's this 10-year-old who lives across the street from us. Anytime my wife and I have technology problems, we call him and he comes over and fixes them for free. You can save a ton of money on repair bills this way.

—*BOB JONES*
SAN DIEGO, CALIFORNIA
19 MOVES

• • • • • • • •

I DON'T REALLY FEEL COMFORTABLE introducing myself to new neighbors. They're the ones who should come over and say hi first. After all, I'm the one invading their territory. Then again, maybe I'm just shy.

—*RANDY FREITIK*
PEORIA, ILLINOIS
2 MOVES

• • • • • • • •

Have a small neighborhood Open House.

—*SHARLANE BLAISE*
PORTLAND,
OREGON
1 MOVE

IF YOU MOVE TO A NEW TOWN, be sure to get out, get involved, and make friends as soon as possible. When I married, I moved from the medium-sized town where I had lived my entire life to a very small, rural town. It was a bit of a culture shock. I never quite adjusted, and we moved back to my hometown eventually.

—*N.J.*
FT. SMITH, ARKANSAS

INTRODUCTION BY AMBUSH

YOU REALLY HAVE TO PUT YOURSELF OUT THERE and make an effort to meet people; you can't expect them to come to you. We moved to a brand-new town in the middle of a cold, snowy February. I was a stay-at-home mom who got really lonely, because none of the neighbors came outside much due to the weather. I spent a lot of time staring out the window, and I began to notice this woman taking regular walks with her stroller at the same time every day. So one day, I waited for her to walk by my house and when she did, I flew out the front door, ran up to her and introduced myself. I invited her inside for coffee and she accepted. We found out that not only were our sons just two months apart, but we were both registered nurses! We've kept in touch for nearly twenty years, but we never would've become friends if I hadn't taken the initiative to introduce myself.

> —*PAMELA BARTH*
> *BAKERSFIELD, CALIFORNIA*
> *7 MOVES*

I MADE IT A POINT TO INTRODUCE MYSELF to all of the neighbors I saw. Then, to meet the others, I just knocked on their doors. Sometimes I made up excuses for why I was knocking, asking if I could borrow a light bulb or if they knew where to put the recycling. Soon after I moved in, I checked out the town's website. It turns out they have a social club, which includes a book club, a gourmet club, and more. I joined and met many people. I considered them  only acquaintances at first, which took the pressure off both them and me. But six months later, many of those acquaintances are developing into true friendships.

> —*SHARON NAYLOR*
> *MADISON, NEW JERSEY*
> *10 MOVES*

TO ADJUST TO A NEW PLACE, don't just sit at home. Go out a lot and try to make new friends. If you are interested in something, join an organization, start working somewhere or go to church. I signed up for college to study journalism—I wanted a degree anyway, and it was a good way to meet people with similar interests.

—*KRISTINA*
SAN ANTONIO, TEXAS
2 MOVES

" The key to making a new place 'yours' is finding a bar, a small bookstore or coffee shop, and a job. Sooner or later, you'll have at least five friends who can make you feel like you belong. "

—*REGINE LABOSSIERE*
LOS ANGELES, CALIFORNIA
5 MOVES

DON'T EXPECT TO FIT RIGHT IN INSTANTLY. When I moved, I found friends right away, but they weren't the ones who ended up being my best friends. Those people took many more months— and even years—to find. It was worth the wait.

—*JENNY W.*
NEW YORK, NEW YORK
3 MOVES

BUY A PIECE OF ART—a beautiful framed photo of a local scene, a coffee table book, whatever—that represents the place you've come from. Leave it out for everyone to see and enjoy in your new home. It makes a good conversation piece and helps you feel connected to old places and friends.

—PAUL W.
MINNEAPOLIS, MINNESOTA
4 MOVES

• • • • • • • • •

YOU NEVER KNOW WHEN YOU'RE GOING to make new friends. Once, my toilet clogged and I didn't have a plunger. So I went next door and knocked and this man with an English accent answered the door. I introduced myself and said, "I just moved in next door and I seem to be having some trouble with plumbing. Do you happen to have a plunger?" He didn't. I didn't know it at the time, but he was heading to the grocery store. I got a knock on my door about a half hour later and he had a plunger for me. He'd bought two—one for his apartment and one for mine.

—ERIN
FRANKLIN, MASSACHUSETTS
6 MOVES

• • • • • • • • •

WHEN YOU MOVE into a new neighborhood, I have always found it helpful to take regular walks around the neighborhood. This gives you the chance to meet your neighbors when they are out and about in their yards.

—ANONYMOUS
NORMAN, OKLAHOMA
1 MOVE

PUT YOUR BEST FOOT FORWARD

I moved in on my neighbor's daughter's wedding day. The reception was being held in their apartment, so they'd had the floors in the outside hallway polished. As I was moving in, my new neighbor came out and started screaming bloody murder at me. "What are you doing?" she yelled. "This is my daughter's big day! You're scuffing up the floors! How could you do this to us?" I was completely taken aback. I mean, how was I supposed to know about her daughter's wedding? Instead of screaming back, however, I calmly asked her how we could resolve the situation. Solution? I ended up moving my stuff in through my front window. It's a good thing I wasn't rude to this woman, too. As it turned out, she was a really long-term resident in the building and a good person. A few months later, while I was at work, a small fire broke out in our building. My neighbor took the time to call information, get my number and leave  me a message at work suggesting I come home and check on my cat. Somehow, I doubt she would've been looking out for me if I'd burned my bridges earlier.

—E.C.
New York, New York
15 MOVES

THE BEST THING I DID was go to work for a temp agency. This allowed me to start paying my bills while working at a number of different companies around town so I could see what I really liked to do.

—*DAN*
BOSTON, MASSACHUSETTS
4 MOVES

• • • • • • • •

The longer you wait to make friends, the harder it is.

—*EDDIE LEE*
STATESBORO,
GEORGIA
3 MOVES

FIND A NATIVE TO TALK TO. I moved from Belgium to Texas to get married and I am lucky because my fiancée tells me where to go to buy things cheaper, what clothes are appropriate to wear, etc. It makes it much easier to adapt.

—*TOM V.M.*
SPRING BRANCH, TEXAS
3 MOVES

• • • • • • • •

BE EXTREMELY FLEXIBLE—and learn to find the humor in almost any situation. Moving from New Jersey to Costa Rica at the age of 23 to take a newspaper job was definitely an eye-opening experience for me. I was single, wide-eyed, and ready for any and all experiences that came my way. But nothing could have fully prepared me for all the subtle and amorphous realities of adjusting to a new culture. Overall, I learned that adjusting is all about flexibility.

—*LAUREN W.*
PHILADELPHIA, PENNSYLVANIA

• • • • • • • •

MAKE SMALL TALK in the laundry room. When you're in there, you know you can always get out quick. You don't want to see their underwear and they don't want to see yours.

—*JONAH*
EVANSTON, ILLINOIS
2 MOVES

YOU'VE GOT TO HAVE THE ABILITY to make new friends to make it through the transitional process. Usually, you can find lots of them through work. Other good ideas include joining groups for activities you enjoy, such as a book club or wine-tasting group.

—*FRAN WILLS*
LITTLETON, COLORADO
4 MOVES

• • • • • • • •

" I don't really care about meeting neighbors. If we happen to cross paths, I'm friendly, and if a relationship develops that's a bonus. "

—*MICHELE HENRY*
TORONTO, ONTARIO, CANADA
3 MOVES

• • • • • • • •

WHEN I MOVE TO NEW PLACES, I make it a policy to knock on people's doors and introduce myself, invite them over for tea or coffee. It helps you feel at home. Once, I moved into this place in New Zealand with a bunch of little old ladies. They were lonely, and it seemed they got loneliest at cocktail time, when in the past they'd be out socializing. So I set up a rotation where we'd have a group happy hour every day. It was cool. My friend and I had fun, and they had a ball.

—*HOLLY CORNETT*
SEATTLE, WASHINGTON
15 MOVES

I MADE A POINT TO STRIKE UP conversations if I saw new faces in the laundry room, hallway or garage of my new apartment building. I met my best friend in the garage when we both realized our bikes had been stolen! We decided to shop for new bicycles together and then we started riding them together. Never underestimate the role your neighbors can play in your life!

—*JEFF MALTZ*
SAN FRANCISCO, CALIFORNIA
8 MOVES

• • • • • • • •

BE CAREFUL ABOUT GETTING TO KNOW your neighbors too well. They can become a nuisance. Once, my niece and I went to the swimming pool and I talked with this lady for a little while. Not long after, she went door-to-door with her three kids looking for me because she was having problems with her ex and was looking for someone to unload on.

—*B.G.*
SAN ANTONIO, TEXAS
5 MOVES

• • • • • • • •

MOST PEOPLE DON'T SPEND ENOUGH TIME visiting the tourist attractions in their own town. People spend thousands of dollars taking far-off vacations but barely know the attractions their own city has to offer. For that reason, a good way to make friends is to ask people the last time they visited a museum in their city, then invite them to come along with you on your first trip.

—*JILL FULLEN*
PITTSBURGH, PENNSYLVANIA
3 MOVES

COMPILE A NEIGHBORHOOD DIRECTORY with house number, family name, family members, email, phone numbers, and pet descriptions and names. I've done this for my block and everyone loves it! The directory makes it easy to call neighbors, arrange for someone to watch your house while you're away, ask your neighbor's teenage son to shovel your walk, etc.

—*SUSAN*
  WESTFIELD, NEW JERSEY
  5 MOVES

• • • • • • • •

BE ALOOF TO YOUR NEIGHBORS to begin with. I have trusted people who I shouldn't have. My neighbor and I never see each other, and that works out fine. I speak to him. He speaks to me. We're friendly, but he tends to his business and me to mine. It's been like this for 18 years.

—*STANLEY O. SHELTON*
  NORMAN, OKLAHOMA
  15 MOVES

• • • • • • • •

WE MOVED FROM A BIG D.C. SUBURB to a small town in Vermont, and it took me the longest time to get used to the fact that every time I met someone in town, they knew where I lived already . . . But I knew more people in two months than I did in several years in Silver Spring, because people were so friendly.

—*J.V.*
  RANDOLPH, VERMONT
  7 MOVES

• • • • • • • •

WE HAVE SOME NOSY NEIGHBORS, so they introduced themselves. It helps that they have a cute daughter.

—*R.*
  RUTHERFORD, NEW JERSEY
  5 MOVES

YOU KNOW YOU'VE MOVED TOO OFTEN WHEN . . .

I GOT A CALL FROM THE PHONE COMPANY, and they asked, verbatim:

"Are you gonna stay where you're at?"
"Who is this?"
"This is the phone company."
"Why do you ask?"
"Because you have a 'T' next to your name."
"What does that mean?"
"You're a transit."

> —J.B.
> TIMONIUM, MARYLAND
> MOVED MANY TIMES

• • • • • • • •

AS A WOMAN, reaching out to other women and making new friends helps me settle into a new place. When I moved from the East Coast to the West Coast, I joined N.O.W. and looked for women of like mind to befriend.

> —B.A.
> PORTLAND, OREGON

Kids and dogs are the best way to meet the neighbors. If you have either, go out for a walk with them. They'll be a conversation-starter.

—*Glenn DiNella*
Birmingham,
Alabama
10 moves

DON'T RUSH INTO MEETING the neighbors. I'm an advocate of putting any kind of meetings like this off until you are completely settled in. You have enough to worry about just getting your new life in order. Those people will still be there when you're ready. And they will understand. Remember, they moved in once, too.

—*Megan Tanner*
Wheeling, West Virginia

• • • • • • • •

WHEN IT COMES TO NEIGHBORS, show that you are the good guy first. I've offered everything from food to free babysitting to picking up something from the store for them. Just extend yourself when you move in to start off on the right foot.

—*Pat Ahern*
Chicago, Illinois
4 moves

• • • • • • • •

IT'S A NICE GESTURE TO WELCOME new people to your neighborhood with a plate of homemade cookies and a note attached. On the note, include your name, phone number and contact information for the important places in town (good restaurants, doctors, the post office, etc.).

—*Kathy McClintic*
Centennial, Colorado
2 moves

• • • • • • • •

DEVELOP A SKILL IN SOMETHING that requires a group to play (tennis, golf, bowling, or bridge, for example). That way, when you move to a new area you can seek out people who play this sport and offer yourself as a sub.

—*Anne Kubas*
Danville, California
7 moves

MOVING TO A NEW PLACE IS NOT EASY, whether it be to the next town or the other side of the world. I've moved about 30 times in my life, and I have learned that it always takes you a year to figure things out. You will go to the Wal-Mart that is 3 miles away in one direction before you learn there is another one 2 blocks away in the other direction. You will have to make efforts to make friends. There is no easy way, so just be prepared and cut yourself some slack.

—*LISA BARNSTROM*
SAN ANTONIO, TEXAS
30 MOVES

• • • • • • • •

" When you move, don't change your whole lifestyle at once. You need to establish some sort of consistency where you aren't uprooting your entire life. "

—*KEVIN*
IOWA CITY, IOWA
10 MOVES

• • • • • • • •

THINK POSITIVE AND TAKE THE INITIATIVE to meet new people by following your interests. I moved from a big city to a small town when I was a sophomore in high school, and that transition was really rough. To adjust, I joined the CPR club, the National Honors Society, and the art club, which allowed me to meet new people and to get a better idea of how the school system worked in my town.

—*MARIA VARGAS*
CASTROVILLE, TEXAS
3 MOVES

STAYING IN TOUCH WITH FAMILY

AFTER WE MOVED AWAY FROM OUR KIDS, my husband and I made an agreement that I could call home whenever I wanted and talk for as long as I wanted. Yes, our phone bills are quite large. But it allows me to feel connected. E-mail is helpful, but sometimes I just needed to hear my daughter's voice!

> —*PAT Q.T.*
> *CALIFORNIA*
> *17 MOVES*

• • • • • • • • •

I HAVE A CELL PHONE, and when I'm thinking of somebody, I'll just call them. I'm so busy that I try to talk on the phone while I'm doing other things. When I'm making dinner and my husband's watching TV, why not talk on the phone?

> —*JAYME*
> *O'FALLON, MISSOURI*
> *2 MOVES*

IT TOOK A WHILE, but eventually we made friends with our neighbors, and also found a church that we both love. I am now a part of a mothers' group at the church and enjoy having their support and advice.

—*AMANDA MILLER*

. . . .

THE KEY FOR ME WAS to get involved. Sports, community-related events, intramurals and clubs give you a small network to expand on.

—*B.J. KLINCK*
PLYMOUTH, MINNESOTA
 *2 MOVES*

. . . .

JOIN ORGANIZATIONS! I found that this was one of the best ways to meet people quickly and survey the city. I joined a political campaign and got a comprehensive view of the city while meeting many different types of locals. Then, I began volunteering at the city aquarium, which allowed me to spend time on the ocean and work with even more wonderful people with similar interests.

—*DAN*
BOSTON, MASSACHUSETTS
4 MOVES

. . . .

GO TO CHURCH, meet people and start forming a support network. Recognize that you will feel out of it for a while, and as you deal with your emotions, understand that these feelings are temporary and it will get better!

—*LORI*
OKLAHOMA CITY, OKLAHOMA
5 MOVES

IT'S CRUCIAL TO FIND A GOOD BARBERSHOP in your new town as soon as possible. Nobody's happy when they don't look good. I have found that the best way to do it is to ask somebody who you think has nice hair where they go.

—*ROB MARINO*
EAST LIVERPOOL, OHIO
🚚 *5 MOVES*

· · · · · · · ·

"I have learned that you need to be very careful about divulging personal information or getting too chummy too quickly with people you first meet, no matter how nice they seem."

—*ANONYMOUS*
BIRMINGHAM, ALABAMA
🚚 *6 MOVES*

· · · · · · · ·

GET A GOOD STREET MAP and spend time as a family discovering where the local grocery stores, schools, parks and churches are. We'd make it into a game when our kids were young. We'd ask questions like, "Who can spot the first 7-11?" or "Where's the nearest Dillards?" to keep things fun.

—*JOE HOLLIMAN*
CENTENNIAL, COLORADO
🚐 *2 MOVES*

I LIVED IN CHICAGO FOR 51 YEARS and then moved to Washington, D.C. I hated it the first year—they didn't have the right kind of hot dogs and it seemed that the women were better looking in my old city. It took me almost 2 years to switch from my barber and doctor in Chicago. I slowly made friends with neighbors and realized you have to create a whole different environment for yourself. If you can get past that first 8 months you'll be fine.

— *B.T.*
DES MOINES, IOWA
3 MOVES

. . . .

IF YOU'VE GOT A DOG, just start walking around and chatting up every dog owner you find. You'll meet a lot of people this way, and it will also help you find the best routes for your dog. These usually end up being the best routes for people like you, with dogs that your dog will also like.

— *DEKE*
SAN DIEGO, CALIFORNIA
13 MOVES

. . . .

EVERY TIME I MOVED, my mother went to the church in the new community and found me a housekeeper or a babysitter, or found out what the best schools were. I was a single mother, and whenever I moved I was going from one huge job to another huge job and just never had time for integrating myself into the community. Having my mother come to the new place with me, even for a small amount of time, gave me a window into the workings of the community.

— *MEL MILLER*
BRISBANE, AUSTRALIA
11 MOVES

Albany-Schenectady-Troy, NY and Harrisburg-Lebanon-Carlisle, PA tied for least stressful cities. Short commutes, low crime and suicide rates were cited.

— *SPERLING'S BEST PLACES*

DON'T BE AFRAID TO TAKE A STAND right off the bat. If you're moving into an apartment, it can be a nightmare if the people above you are loud. In one of my apartments, the people started blaring their music the second night I was there. I ran up the stairs and let them know I wouldn't stand for my apartment shaking due to their music. After that, I never had a problem.

—*JEAN ROBERTSON*
GLENVIEW, ILLINOIS
3 MOVES

* * * * * * * *

FIND THREE OR FOUR PLACES that are important to you, like a shopping mall, bagel shop, and cafe, and become a regular there so people know you. Build a relationship with those stores; that way you'll feel like you're part of a community and you'll create a routine of external things outside of your place.

—*ROHAN THAKUR*
MINNEAPOLIS, MINNESOTA
4 MOVES

* * * * * * * *

TALK ABOUT FRESH START! I moved from Los Angeles to Brooklyn. Upon arrival I faced an empty five-room apartment with a folding chair, a cardboard box desk and my laptop wet with tears. But if you give a girl a jigsaw and screw gun, she can build a new life. I built my own bookshelves, stereo area customized to house my rather large vinyl collection, and a large worktable complete with lots of flat storage. I found that the physical labor of creating a new place facilitated a very memorable healing.

—*HAWLEY HUSSEY*
BROOKLYN, NEW YORK
10 MOVES

Organize a block party to get to know your neighbors.

—*SUSAN WESTFIELD, NEW JERSEY*
5 MOVES

BUY LOTS OF SMALL SOUVENIRS that you could use as gifts when you introduce yourself to new neighbors or go to the home of new friends. When I left Vermont, I bought a bunch of maple sugar candies. They were cheap—just a couple bucks each—but in a cute little maple leaf shape and nice box. I included the candy with a nice note for the new neighbors. It helped break the ice.

—*N. CLARK*
HOUSTON, TEXAS
3 MOVES

• • • • • • • •

I'VE MOVED TO 17 COUNTRIES in the past 35 years. And I've lived on every continent. The hardest part about moving: the aloneness. My husband and I are very close, but often he was working so I was left at home alone. It usually took several months for me to get active with church groups or other volunteer organizations where I would meet people. Once I got involved, I made lots of friends. Then, I had to schedule time for myself!

—*PAT Q.T.*
CALIFORNIA
17 MOVES

• • • • • • • •

WHEN OUR NEW NEIGHBORS MOVED IN, they left a heart-shaped candy cane ornament on our front doorknob with a note attached that read, "Merry Christmas from your new neighbors." I thought it was a totally sweet, creative way to introduce themselves.

—*WREN JOHNSON*
CENTENNIAL, COLORADO
5 MOVES

THE FIRST TIME SOMEBODY STOPPED ME on the street to ask for directions, I just couldn't believe it. It sounds so silly, but I felt so proud that I knew what he was talking about and could give him perfect directions off the top of my head. I thought to myself, "I must really live here!"

—*JEANIE*
MINNEAPOLIS, MINNESOTA
5 MOVES

· · · · · · · · ·

66 I'm not sure this is the way you're supposed to do it, but I usually introduce myself to neighbors when one of my teenagers runs over their mailbox. 99

—*W. BRUCE CAMERON*
SANTA MONICA, CALIFORNIA
12 MOVES

· · · · · · · · ·

I'M AN EPISCOPAL PRIEST. My new church proved an incredibly valuable resource for most of the transition, including finding a good place to live. The members put together a poll that ascertained everything from the best car mechanic to liquor store to firewood dealer and optometrist. I still have the three-page list and will use it for years.

—*MARTHA ENGLERT*
MADISON, WISCONSIN

GET OUT OF THE HOUSE and take some rides to familiarize yourself with the new roads. I would get in the car on a Sunday afternoon and just drive around a bit and see what was where. Don't forget to bring a map.

—*PHIL LYNCH*
PITTSBURGH, PENNSYLVANIA
 *2 MOVES*

• • • • • • • •

I MADE A POINT OF CHECKING OUT ALL THE BARS. I would go have a drink at the different ones till I'd narrowed it down to a couple that I really liked. Then I went into those bars and really chatted with the bartenders, made time to meet the people who were regulars. I made some good friends that way and also ended up with one place that felt like a "second home" to me.

—*CARL M.*
MINNEAPOLIS, MINNESOTA
 *10 MOVES*

• • • • • • • •

I SPENT THE FIRST FEW WEEKS really throwing myself into my work, which is a good idea when you have a new job anyway. Through work, I started to meet people and make friends.

—*TRENT S.*
TUSCALOOSA, ALABAMA
3 MOVES

• • • • • • • •

WHEN I MOVED TO TEXAS, I really enjoyed jogging around the neighborhood to get acclimated to my surroundings. It was great, because I found lots of local restaurants that way, and it also gave me a chance to chat with neighbors. I met my first friends there as I was stretching outside my house before a run!

—*ANNE SMALLEY*
WOODBURY, NEW JERSEY

When decorating your home, know this: Color holds the responsibility of solving the majority of design problems . . . Color can make a room livable.

—*STRAIGHT TALK ON DECORATING*

WHEN MY TRUCK SHOWED UP, the movers wouldn't bring my boxes to the third floor even though I pre-paid for that. Three "tough guys" from my new neighborhood saw I was having difficulty and came over to see what was up. They suggested to the truckers that if I said I pre-paid for this I probably did and they should bring the boxes up. They quite literally stood there smoking for the entire process.

—HAWLEY HUSSEY
BROOKLYN, NEW YORK
🚚 10 MOVES

• • • • • • • •

  66 It helped that I met a guy
soon after arriving—a guy
that I liked and made out
with all the time. 99

—ANONYMOUS
ARLINGTON, VIRGINIA

• • • • • • • •

IF YOU'RE A DOG LOVER (or can stand them), offer to watch your neighbor's pet if they go out of town. If you see them outside playing with the dog, just throw out the idea in case they ever go on vacation. Every pet owner knows it's hard to figure out what to do with your dog when you go away. If you make it easier for someone else, you'll be in good graces for a while.

—RUSSELL SCHMIDT
ARLINGTON HEIGHTS, ILLINOIS
🚚 5 MOVES

MAINTAIN YOUR SENSE OF SELF, especially in a new environment. When I was 13 years old, my family moved from Lynchburg, Virginia, where I was very popular, to Singapore. I couldn't have felt more alien or out of place. But I soon learned that I was still the same person I was before, and my personality came out, and I made new friends.

— *DAVID MULLIN*
  PHILADELPHIA, PENNSYLVANIA

. . . .

DON'T BE SHY. Don't be lazy or come up with excuses to stay home and stare at the TV, watching shows that make you dumber. If you have to kick your own arse to motivate yourself, kick it! It will pay off. Sooner rather than later, you'll feel less lost and less alone. And you'll discover things about yourself and your new home in the process.

— *TINA MITRO*

. . . .

IF YOU LIVE IN AN APARTMENT and get friendly with the neighbors, it's inevitable that you will always owe them something. I was nice to one guy in my last apartment building and every time he went out of town (several times a month) he'd ask me to take care of his bird. It was a real hassle.

— *S. LIVINGSTON*
  CHICAGO, ILLINOIS
  4 MOVES

. . . .

CREATE AN ONLINE GROUP. Our neighborhood has a Yahoo group and mailing list. This helps us keep track of when kids will be trick-or-treating, news of any sick neighbors or new babies, etc.

— *SUSAN*
  WESTFIELD, NEW JERSEY
  5 MOVES

Stay away from gossip. Just lie back and find out things for yourself.

— *KATE CRONE*
  GREEN BAY,
  WISCONSIN

I HEARD SOMETHING ON THE RADIO that I believe is really true: It takes some people five years to adjust to a new place after they move. You might think this sounds ridiculous, but it was at least five years before I finally stopped saying stuff like, "Oh, we're going home to visit next weekend" after my move.

—*L.A.*
CLEVELAND, OHIO
11 MOVES

. . . .

WE BOTH GOT VERY INVOLVED IN THE TOWN as soon as we could. My husband is on the borough council and I have been a committee person for a political party in our area. We both also do lots of work with our church. By getting involved right away, you get to know so many people so much quicker than you would if you just sat at home all day.

—*DIANE ROSE SMITH*
HARMONY, PENNSYLVANIA

More Wisdom: Good Stuff That Doesn't Fit Anywhere Else

*W*ell, well. Here you are, sitting in your new place, new friends leaving messages and old ones sending e-mails, pictures hanging right where you want them . . . and, best of all, you haven't lost this book. Congratulations. You might not move again for a while, but you have to admit, despite all the hard work, it's worth it to see a new place and meet new people. Someday, you might get tired of your place and long to move again. But until then, here's some added advice, and may your future journeys bring you much joy and adventure.

IN THE PAST I HAVE LIKED MOVING, because it meant a fresh start. Now I'm tired and old and don't want to carry things anymore.

—*SARAH*
SEATTLE, WASHINGTON
15 MOVES

EXPECT THE UNEXPECTED.

—*M.A.*
BARLING, ARKANSAS
3 MOVES

YOU WILL SURVIVE MOVING by learning to love it! Moving is a good way to clean out and organize your life. Packing forces you to go through the junk that has built up since your last move, and unpacking forces you to put everything in order. Plus, you get to meet new people, and get a change of environment. It is always nice, I find, to have a clean slate and start over.

—*MELISSA MANFRO*
PHILADELPHIA, PENNSYLVANIA
4 MOVES

Moving is fine if it's happening to someone else . . . particularly someone you don't like.

—*CASSANDRA FOX*
FAIRFAX STATION, VIRGINIA
MOVED A LOT

• • • • • • • •

TAKE A GOOD LOOK BEFORE YOU LEAP! I will never forget the sinking feeling of "what have I done?" when I arrived in Alaska. It was a lifestyle and environment totally foreign to what I was used to. Make sure you know what you're getting yourself into before the decision is final. You'll be glad you did!

—*L.A.*
PALMER, ALASKA
7 MOVES

• • • • • • • •

WHEN YOU MOVE, accept your new place as your home. Know that you have to make it the best possible situation, for however long you're going to be living there. When we moved to Hawaii I thought, "Oh my gosh, we're 5,000 miles away from home." But then I realized Hawaii *was* my home because my husband and family were with me. Don't expect everything to be perfect. Just accept it as your new home.

—*NORA HAMMOND*
LOUISVILLE, KENTUCKY

RECENTLY I MOVED CROSS-COUNTRY, something I had been planning on doing my entire life, and through the experience realized one thing that can be relevant to any move—whether carefully planned or luck of the draw: Do not expect too much. If you do, you will end up like me and move back to the other side of the country wondering what went wrong.

—NOAH SHUSSETT
BROOKLYN, NEW YORK
4 MOVES

• • • • • • • •

DON'T BUY MORE JUNK when you just got rid of your trash. When we moved from Arizona, we had a yard sale to get rid of all the lawn ornaments we'd never use in Chicago. Less than a week after we came here, my wife went to someone else's lawn sale and loaded up on more stuff that has been sitting in our garage for three years.

—MATT
SKOKIE, ILLINOIS
7 MOVES

In 2004, Atlanta was the top U.S. destination city for the fourth year in a row. Rounding out the top five: Dallas, Houston, Chicago and New York.

—U-HAUL

• • • • • • • •

" People who move a lot are never introverts. We can't be. "

—JOHN W.
LONGMEADOW, MASSACHUSETTS

WHEN MOVING TO A NEW CITY, new job, or even just a new apartment, the goal is to have a fearless attitude. Commit and go for it! You only live once, so you are responsible for making things happen. Be prepared for a few lonely nights spent with Ben and Jerry's. It is all part of it. You'll appreciate the new people that you meet so much more after getting through the lonely periods.

—*MARY*
NEW YORK, NEW YORK
7 MOVES

• • • • • • • •

THE BEST THING TO DO when you're moving is to find a good support network wherever you're going. I'd never met them before, but it turned out that I had cousins in my new town. The great thing about family is that no matter how distant, they'll most likely be willing to help. With these connections in hand, I was able to stay in the area for free for a couple of weeks and check out apartments and neighborhoods to my heart's content without the usual pressure. I also got great advice from people who knew the area, and had some much needed company those first lonely days in a new city.

—*JACKLYN BEEBE*
WASHINGTON, DC
4 MOVES

• • • • • • • •

GETTING MY DOG SETTLED, figuring out where to put her bed and food dishes, made it feel like home right away. Also, having a dog makes it easier to meet new people.

—*CRYSTAL J.*
DES MOINES, IOWA
10 MOVES

Best cities for entrepreneurs: Minneapolis-St. Paul, Washington, DC, Atlanta, Ft. Lauderdale, Salt Lake City-Ogden.

—*ENTREPRENEUR*

BE NICE TO PEOPLE. One day, they will keep stuff for you, take stuff permanently off your hands, or let you stay with them on the road to your "final" destination.

> —*REGINE LABOSSIERE*
> *LOS ANGELES, CALIFORNIA*
> *5 MOVES*

• • • • • • • •

WHEN IT COMES TO DECORATING the new house, give up early, men, because your wife has control. I'm a hunter, and over the years, as we've moved up from a mobile home to a 2,800-square-foot plus basement house, it's gone from me being allowed to keep my trophy heads everywhere to them being confined to a small office. In fact, it seems like the more house we get, the less space I have!

> —*KERRY MCINTOSH*
> *CASTLE ROCK, COLORADO*
> *12 MOVES*

• • • • • • • •

TREAT YOURSELF. Pick out a few rugs for yourselves and some comfy cushions for your new rooms.

> —*E.T.*
> *PORTLAND, MAINE*
> *4 MOVES*

• • • • • • • •

A HOME IS WHAT YOU MAKE IT. When I first saw my home, I thought it was really ugly. But my husband liked it and told me, "We can make it what we want it to be." And we did. We painted the inside and outside a different color, did landscaping, mosaic-tiled the kitchen and the bathroom, and painted a mural. Now we have a house that is special to us.

> —*LANAN SHELTON*
> *AUSTIN, TEXAS*
> *10 MOVES*

Expect the worst, compound it by a factor of 1000, grit your teeth and bear it.

> —*ANNMARIE LOCKHART*
> *ENGLEWOOD, NEW JERSEY*
> *8 MOVES*

MAKE THE MOST OF IT

We moved from our beautiful first home, which we owned, to another city where increased cost of living forced us to rent. The only place we could find was sitting on the corner of a busy intersection by a university. Down the street were all of the fraternity and sorority houses.

We could have whined and moaned and been like, "Poor me!" After all, our three kids were in kindergarten, first and second grade. Not exactly the ideal age to expose them to college life. Instead, we decided to look for the silver lining and make the most of our situation.

We found instant babysitters in the college students, who frequently stopped by to talk or give our kids presents. We watched the university football games from our upstairs window, because the stadium was across the street. The annual homecoming parade was also excellent. I truly believe our positive attitude turned something that could've been unpleasant into lots of really fond memories.

    —BARB ZAHN
    FRANKTOWN, COLORADO
    10 MOVES

WHEN MOVING OUT OF MY HOUSE for the first time, I overlooked the importance of an air conditioner. I was always cold in my parents' house when the central air was on, so I thought it wouldn't be a big deal that there was no air in my first apartment. The first hot day of the summer, I called my parents and begged for a window unit, because a third-floor apartment in Chicago heat is miserable in the summer.

—*ABBY*
  CHICAGO, ILLINOIS
  🚚 *1 MOVE*

• • • • • • • •

I WOULDN'T RECOMMEND getting married, moving to another state and starting a new job all in the same week.

—*SARAH R.*
  BOSTON, MASSCHUSETTS
  🚚 *16 MOVES*

• • • • • • • •

THERE'S AN OLD SAYING that goes, "You can pick your nose, but you can't pick your neighbors." However, to reduce your chances of getting bad neighbors, don't buy in an area where there are lots of rental houses.

—*BOB JONES*
  SAN DIEGO, CALIFORNIA
  🚚 *19 MOVES*

According to the 2000 U.S. Census, suburbs were growing at a faster rate than major cities, and the West and South were growing faster than the Northeast and Midwest.

—*MSN HOUSE & HOME*

How did I survive my move? I drank.

—*A Canadian*
Washington, DC

IT HELPS TO LOOK AROUND before you settle in. I rented a furnished apartment for the first nine months. Then, when I knew I would stay, I chose an apartment close to a bus stop and subway; across the street from a grocery store; and a block from the laundromat. I had all my basic needs within a one-block proximity. After signing a lease, I ordered furniture that was small and returnable if it didn't fit. I also surveyed the area for all my basic amenities.

—*N.L.*
New York, New York
6 MOVES

• • • • • • • •

"Why stress out? What is the worst that can happen?! You can break something or get sweaty."

—*Zinnia*
Hoboken, New Jersey
7 MOVES

• • • • • • • •

I DON'T KNOW THAT YOU EVER really get over moving. You look back at those memories and they're there. They're a part of your life. Just be optimistic about the new place. Know that there are happy memories in the old place, but there's also a happy future ahead.

—*Christian Batog*
Franklin, Massachusetts
6 MOVES

DON'T TREAT YOUR APARTMENT as if it's your house. You are probably not going to be there very long, so don't spend too much time or money improving the place. We painted the first few apartments we lived in at our own expense. And then, for various reasons, we moved out shortly after that. It's just not worth it. You can learn to live with a green living room. Believe me.

—*KEVIN L. MCCARTHY*
PITTSBURGH, PENNSYLVANIA
9 MOVES

• • • • • • • •

DO NOT LET THE STRESS OF MOVING cause you to be rude to those who you love the most, and those who love *you* the most. I was so mean one year that when the next year rolled around, no one wanted to help me. But I don't really blame them. I was a real pain in the ass!

—*DACODA K.*
NEW YORK, NEW YORK
2 MOVES

• • • • • • • •

AFTER THE MOVE, implement a new system so that you do not accumulate so much stuff this time around. When you receive a sweater for Christmas, donate two old ones. I do not have odd mugs, plastic cups, dish towels or beach towels. I have two matching mugs. I have one set of silverware. Once a set starts missing pieces or is damaged, I donate it. I never have to search for anything in my kitchen, because it is organized and matches. It's ok to keep tossing things after the move. Don't feel like you owe the item a home because you took the effort to move it. Keep lightening your load.

—*JILL MARIE DAVIS*
WEEHAWKEN, NEW JERSEY
12 MOVES

U-Haul is the world's largest single-brand Yellow Pages advertiser.

—*U-HAUL*

THE ONE THING I WISH I had when I moved was a videotape of my old house, family, and friends. It would have helped me deal with homesickness, and I would have been able to show it to my friends and share that part of me.

—*TAYLOR MCGINLEY*
LAGUNA HILLS, CALIFORNIA
🚚 *2 MOVES*

• • • • • • • •

I WOULDN'T HAVE SURVIVED my first move without my parents—aka, my personal mover (dad) and interior designer (mom). They took me to IKEA to buy all of my new furniture and carted it to my new home and put it all together for me. They also brought all of my belongings from home. They put up all of the curtains and pictures on the wall, and listened to my whiney phone calls about leaks and electrical problems. Spoiled rotten? Most definitely. But that is what parents are for!

—*KATY WARD*
QUEENS, NEW YORK
🚚 *6 MOVES*

• • • • • • • •

HOW HAVE MY WIFE AND I SURVIVED 10 moves around the country? Easily. We eagerly anticipated every move, focusing entirely on the fun and adventure and refusing to dwell on our previous locale. Rearview mirrors are good in cars but bad in life.

—*DOUGLAS S. LOONEY*
BOULDER, COLORADO
🚚 *10 MOVES*

You thought *your* relocation to a new home was expensive . . . Plans for a new Yankee Stadium, just a short walk from the original, will cost an estimated $750 million.

—*NEW YORK TIMES*

I'VE MOVED AROUND THE UNITED STATES and throughout the world. It gets easier every time. I gained more insight and experience with each move. Eventually I learned that any difficulty can be handled and any problem solved. And, most importantly, I enjoyed myself.

—*NANCY*
BRUSSELS, BELGIUM,
6 MOVES

• • • • • • • •

" Go through your things every year and throw out things or give them away. If you haven't used something in a year or two, get rid of it. "

—*LORAINE*
BOSTON, MASSACHUSETTS
5 MOVES

• • • • • • • •

FAMILY IS FAMILY. When they are all in one place, that's what makes a home.

—*ANONYMOUS*
CUSHING, OKLAHOMA
15 MOVES

SPECIAL THANKS

Thanks to our intrepid "headhunters" for going out to find so many "movers" from around the country with interesting advice to share:

Jennifer Batog	Natasha Lambropoulos	Beshaleba Rodell
Jennifer Blaise	Nicole Lessin	Graciela Sholander
Jennifer Bright Reich	Robin Lofton	Laura Roe Stevens
Jennifer Byrne	Ken McCarthy	Andrea Syrtash
Scott Deckman	Christina Orlovsky	Matt Villano
Elizabeth Edwardsen	Peter Ramirez	Jade Walker
Lisa Jaffe Hubbell	William Ramsey	Sara Walker
Shannon Hurd	Kazz Regelman	Joanne Wolfe

Thanks, too, to our editorial advisor Alys R. Yablon. And thanks to our assistant, Miri Greidi, for her yeoman's work at keeping us all organized.

The real credit for this book, of course, goes to all the people whose experiences and collective wisdom make up this guide. There are too many of you to thank individually, of course, but you know who you are. Thanks for sharing.

CREDITS

Page 5: MSN House & Home, "Where Are You Going?"

Page 6: *The Everything Homeselling Book*, Ruth Rejnis, ©2000, Adams Media Corporation

Page 9: U-Haul International, Inc.

Page 10: *Forbes Magazine*, "Best Cities for Singles," 2002 http://www.forbes.com/static_html/singles/2002.html

Page 13: CNN.com, "Big Bucks or Lofty Lifestyle," September 17, 2004

Page 14: Rosetta Hammond is a real estate broker

Page 20: *The Unofficial Guide to Buying a Home*, Alan Perlis and Beth Bradley, ©2004 by Robert Sehlinger, Wiley Publishing House, Inc.

Page 22: *The Everything Homeselling Book*, Ruth Rejnis, ©2000, Adams Media Corporation

Page 25: U-Haul.com

Page 26: About.com, "Millions in Tax Checks Returned to IRS" http://usgov-info.about.com/library/weekly/aa110301a.htm

Page 29: HomeDepotMoving.com, "Moving with Plants"

Page 40: *The Unofficial Guide to Buying a Home*, Alan Perlis and Beth Bradley, ©2004 by Robert Sehlinger, Wiley Publishing House, Inc.

Page 43: U-Haul.com

Page 50: *The One-Minute Organizer*, Donna Smallin, ©2004 by Donna Marie Smallin, Smalley Publishing

Page 57: *The Everything Homeselling Book*, Ruth Rejnis, ©2000, Adams Media Corporation

Page 59: *The One-Minute Organizer*, Donna Smallin, ©2004 by Donna Marie Smallin, Smalley Publishing

Page 67: HomeDepotMoving.com, "Tips on Garage Sales"

Page 73: Susie Walton is a "Redirecting Children's Behavior" course instructor

Page 74: Ehow.com, "How to Help Your Child Make Friends at a New School"

Page 76: Susie Walton is a "Redirecting Children's Behavior" course instructor

Page 81: Pediatrics Health Monitor, "Moving to a New Home? Have Children? Read This!" http://www.healthmonitor.com/TEMPRES/ped060201DWF1.htm

Page 83: W. Bruce Cameron is a nationally syndicated columnist and auther of *8 Simple Rules for Dating My Teenage Daughter* and *How to Remodel a Man*

Page 89: Delta Airlines

Page 94: Delta Airlines

Page 99: Moving.com, How to Pack Like a Pro

Page 101: Mitch Hedberg, Comedian

Page 106: Moving.com, Motorcycle Guide

Page 111: *The Everything Homeselling Book*, Ruth Rejnis, ©2000, Adams
    Media Corporation

Page 115: U-Haul.com

Page 131: US Census Bureau

Page 139: HomeDepotMoving.com, "On Moving Day"

Page 140: Sperling's Best Places, "America's Most Challenging Cities to
    Navigate" http://www.bestplaces.net/docs/studies/NavCities.aspx

Page 152: Sperling's Best Places, "America's Most (and Least) Stressful
    Cities" http://www.bestplaces.net/docs/studies/NavCities.aspx

Page 163: U-Haul International, Inc.

Page 167: *The Unofficial Guide to Buying a Home*, Alan Perlis and Beth
    Bradley, ©2004 by Robert Sehlinger, Wiley Publishing House, Inc.

Page 170: *The One-Minute Organizer*, Donna Smallin, ©2004 by Donna
    Marie Smallin, Smalley Publishing

Page 193: Apartments.com, Moving Center, "Five Calls You Absolutely Must
    Make Within Twenty-Four Hours of Moving In"

Page 213: Sperling's Best Places, "America's Most (and Least) Stressful
    Cities" http://www.bestplaces.net/docs/studies/NavCities.aspx

Page 216: W. Bruce Cameron is a nationally syndicated columnist and auther
    of *8 Simple Rules for Dating My Teenage Daughter* and *How to
    Remodel a Man*

Page 217: *Straight Talk on Decorating*, by Lynette Jennings, ©2002,
    Meredith Press

Page 223: U-Haul, March 16, 2004

Page 224: *Entrepreneur and D&B's 2003 Best Cities for Entrepreneurs*
    http://www.entrepreneur.com/bestcities/0,5271,,00.html?category=i
    nktomi

Page 227: MSN House & Home, "Where Are You Going?"

Page 229: U-Haul.com

Page 230: *New York Times*, September 5, 2004

HELP YOUR FRIENDS SURVIVE!

Order extra copies of *How to Survive A Move,* or one of our other books:

Check your local bookstore or www.hundredsofheads.com, or order here.

Please send me:

_____ copies of How to Survive A Move (@$13.95)

_____ copies of How to Survive Your Marriage (@$13.95)

_____ copies of How to Survive Your Baby's First Year (@$12.95)

_____ copies of How to Survive Dating (@$12.95)

_____ copies of How to Survive Your Freshman Year (@$12.95)

Please add $3.00 for shipping and handling for one book, and $1.00 for each additional book. Georgia residents add 4% sales tax. Kansas residents add 5.3% sales tax. Payment must accompany orders. Please allow 3 weeks for delivery.

My check for $_____ is enclosed.

Please charge my __ Visa __ MasterCard __ American Express

Name _____

Organization _____

Address _____

City/State/Zip _____

Phone _____E-mail _____

Credit card # _____

Exp. Date _____Signature _____

Please make checks payable to HUNDREDS OF HEADS BOOKS, INC.

Please fax to 212-937-2220, or mail to:

HUNDREDS OF HEADS BOOKS, INC.
#230
2221 Peachtree Road, Suite D
Atlanta, Georgia 30309

www.hundredsofheads.com

HELP WRITE THE NEXT Hundreds of Heads™ SURVIVAL GUIDE!

Tell us your story about a life experience, and what lesson you learned from it. If we use your story in one of our books, we'll send you a free copy. Use this card or visit www.hundredsofheads.com.

Here's my story/advice on surviving

❏ **A New Job** (years working:_____ profession/job:_____)

❏ **A Move** (# times you've moved:_____) ❏ **A Diet** (# lbs. lost in best diet: _____)

❏ **A Teenager** (ages/sexes of your children: _____)

❏ **Divorce** (times married: _____ times divorced:_____)

❏ _____ **Other topic** (you pick)

Name _____City/State: _____

❏ Use my name ❏ Use my initials only ❏ Anonymous

(Note: Your entry in the book may also include city/state and the descriptive information above.)

How should we contact you *(this will not be published or shared):*

e-mail: _____ other: _____

Please mail to:

HUNDREDS OF HEADS BOOKS, INC.
#230
2221 Peachtree Road, Suite D
Atlanta, Georgia 30309

Your story/advice:

ABOUT THE EDITORS

JAMIE ALLEN:
Jamie Allen is an editor and "chief headhunter" for the HUNDREDS OF HEADS survival guide series. He has worked as a producer in television news, and he spent five years as a senior writer and editor for CNN.com. Jamie survives his family's moves by pretending to know exactly what he is doing at all times, even when he doesn't have a clue. He lives in Atlanta with his wife and two children.

KAZZ REGELMAN:
Kazz Regelman has moved to new houses, cities, states, countries, and even continents more times than she can count. Her family relocated several times while she was young, and she has no idea how to answer when people ask, "Where are you from?" Once, as an adult with no place to stay in between houses, she snuck into her office late at night and slept in the shadow of the copy machine. (She was not comfortable.) Kazz graduated from Princeton University, studied in Taiwan on a Fulbright Scholarship, and worked in Tokyo as a correspondent for *Variety Magazine*. She lives in San Francisco with her husband and daughter.

VISIT WWW.HUNDREDSOFHEADS.COM

Do you have something interesting to say about marriage, your in-laws, dieting, holding a job, or one of life's other challenges?

 Help humanity—share your story!

✔ Get published in our next book!

✔ Find out about the upcoming titles in the HUNDREDS OF HEADS™ survival guide series!

✔ Read up-to-the-minute advice on many of life's challenges!

✔ Sign up to become an interviewer for one of the next HUNDREDS OF HEADS™ survival guides!

Visit www.hundredsofheads.com today!

Other Books from HUNDREDS OF HEADS™ BOOKS

HOW TO SURVIVE YOUR FRESHMAN YEAR . . . by Hundreds of Sophomores, Juniors, and Seniors Who Did (and some things to avoid, from a few dropouts who didn't)™ (April 2004; ISBN 0-9746292-0-0)

HOW TO SURVIVE DATING . . . by Hundreds of Happy Singles Who Did (and some things to avoid, from a few broken hearts who didn't)™ (October 2004; ISBN 0-9746292-1-9)

HOW TO SURVIVE YOUR BABY'S FIRST YEAR . . . by Hundreds of Happy Parents Who Did (and some things to avoid, from a few who barely made it)™ (January 2005; ISBN 0-9746292-2-7)

HOW TO SURVIVE YOUR MARRIAGE . . . by Hundreds of Happy Couples Who Did (and some things to avoid, from a few ex-spouses who didn't)™ (February 2005; 0-9746292-4-3)

HOW TO SURVIVE YOUR TEENAGER . . . by Hundreds of Still-Sane Parents Who Did (and some things to avoid, from a few whose kids drove them nuts)™ (Spring 2005; ISBN 0-9746292-3-5)